THORNTON WILDER

THORNTON WILDER

≺ Helmut Papajewski

Translated by John Conway ≻

Frederick Ungar Publishing Co. / New York

Translated from the German *Thornton Wilder*
© 1965 Athenaum Verlag GmbH. Frankfurt am Main
Published by arrangement with the original publishers
Copyright © 1968 by Frederick Ungar Publishing Co., Inc.
Printed in the United States of America
Library of Congress Catalog Card Number: 68-25897

Foreword

OF THE TWO creative orientations that for decades have essentially determined American literature, the more outstanding is the one that stresses the independent character of that literature. The European reader has sought clarification by contrasting this orientation with creative conditions and atmospheres that are different. And through the interpretation of the phenomena of modern life, an interpretation sometimes not so different from the European's view (think of the literature of existentialism)—he has found a confirmation of his own ideas.

The following analysis of the novels and plays of Thornton Wilder, then, is not in the nature of an apologia. Wilder's present reputation in Europe, especially in Germany, rests on a strong foundation. The European finds the study of Wilder's work all the more inviting in that it shows marks of traditions common to both Europe and America, yet without making Wilder appear a traditionalist.

I owe thanks to my collaborator Maria Wickert, whose knowledge of ancient literatures elucidated many a context until her death in October 1959. I wish to thank Rainer Lengeler, who contributed many improvements to the text and its coherence, and I am indebted also to Inge Leimberg, from whose feeling for literary form Chapters Four, Five and Nine have especially benefited.

H. P.

Contents

⤙ 1 ⤚

The Cabala

AFTER his first long sojourn in Europe, which he spent mainly at the American Academy in Rome, Thornton Wilder in 1926 brought out his novel *The Cabala*. The title has something mystifying about it; it can relate either to the theosophic interpretation of the religious scriptures of the Jews, or to a conspiratorial society of a kind not very different from that which had extensive power for a time in seventeenth-century England.

Notwithstanding all the secretiveness, Wilder does not keep the reader waiting long for a hint of the society's aims. We soon learn that it is a kind of ultraconservative clique exercising a not inconsiderable influence in the clerical and political world. For the views of its members as to a policy program, there is by no means a common denominator. Wilder solves the question of how to introduce the reader by a narrative technique of gradually stronger fade-ins and flashbacks, whereby the real character of this secret society slowly becomes manifest. Blair, who calls the attention of his American friends and travel companions to this organization, mentions only a few adherents, in particular Miss Grier, who introduces him to the circle. By this means he becomes acquainted with two more members of the Cabala.

Acquaintance with other members, who are to play a decisive role in the course of the story, is reserved for a third stage of his initiation.

The occasional mention of the person of Astrée-Luce is not of great significance at this stage; this figure will become fully distinct only with the reports in the later chapters. The principal persons determine the character of the major sections of the book. Even the chapter titles are taken from the names of the major actors in the drama: Marcantonio, Princess D'Espoli, the Cardinal, and Astrée-Luce. In the concluding section—as she had already done in Book One—Miss Grier appears as proxy for the Cabala, and the leading role is played by the first-person narrator. Thus there has emerged a plot framework, a device for which Wilder was also later to show a great preference.

In an old world and in a society sworn to preserve it, two Americans play deciding roles. One is Miss Grier, a kind of dictator. The other is the confidant of all, the narrator himself, who has an argumentative bent and a certain aloofness toward the society's proceedings. This distant attitude relates primarily to the political program in the narrow sense. In the action itself he appears as a messenger, with all a messenger's functions, large and small. That these functions are not of a subordinate technical kind follows from the mythological appellation which is later conferred on him. Of secondary importance are persons such as Madame Agarapoulos, who is to be regarded as the representative of an undoubtedly subordinate level of Roman society. Likewise, Miss Roy, who played a part at the beginning of the novel, is reintroduced by Wilder in order to perform subordinate functions of the plot.

The narrator is the principal character, who holds together the novel's framework, consisting of an introductory chapter and an Epilogue as well as the three episodic chapters of the plot. These latter are similar in their basic structure: a human being with the will to self-destruction leaps to his death with a cry of despair on his lips.

The novel's outer framework is tightly constructed. All the episodes take place in Rome within the span of a year. This concentration of design is also served by the way the author launches directly into the action. On the day following his arrival in Rome the narrator, together with the young Harvard archaeologist Blair, goes to the leader of the Cabala, Miss Grier. The two decisive invitations immediately follow, which, in Book Two, set the train of events in motion and carry the plot to further development. The invitations are to Tivoli and to the Villa Colonna. Here at an early stage, then, are brief references to the background of the plot. The residence stands for the preservation of things Roman. It is the house that Maecenas is supposed to have given Horace, the villa to which the latter makes allusion in these lines from the *Carmina* (I.vii, 12–14):

> . . . domus Albuniae resonantis
> Et praeceps Anio ac Tiburni locus et uda
> Mobilibus pomaria rivis.[1]

The historical continuity becomes clear when it is recalled that the Colonnas are more or less identifiable with the leading families and the events of Roman history during the Middle Ages and the Renaissance.

There is a good deal of snobbery in these allusions to past history. For the novel they are of course an important structural element, the key to which lies in the words of Cardinal Vaini: "Who can understand love unless he has loved without response? . . . You know, there is for every human being one text in the Bible that can shake him, just as every building has a musical note that can overthrow it."[2] With ancient, medieval, and Renaissance elements, each dominant in its turn, the Cabala's conduct will be challenged.

Wilder has here drawn a very tight time span for his novel. In Tivoli and the Villa Colonna the dialogue and action are to be fixed within the first week. One week later the principal character has the fateful conversation with Marcantonio that is to lead to the latter's death. Fourteen days after the action is launched comes the first catastrophe.

Later in the story Wilder becomes more sparing in his assignment of dates to these events. In Book Three the dating of incidents is quite sporadic, and at times slightly inaccurate. Meanwhile the narrator's acquaintances develop comparatively rapidly. The narrator thereby fulfills an essential function that has its source in mythology. Toward the novel's end Miss Grier tells the story of a Dutchman who was the reincarnation of Mercury, and she expresses to the principal character her suspicion that, following the Dutchman's death, he has become the new embodiment of Mercury. He has thus become the messenger of the gods, who establishes their contacts with humans, but who also has the task of escorting the dead to Hades. The significance of this latter function lies, of course, in the fact that each of the three central stories has a tragic issue.

In fixing the time of day for his events Wilder is very exact, because this detail is used for atmospheric effect. Nighttime receives a very conscious preference. All important events take place in the evening or at night. Late at night—"in the proud middle of the night" [3]—the narrator arrives in Rome. He has his last conversation about the Cabala at night,[4] and at the end he leaves Italy during the night.[5] All other events that have any kind of importance for the plot likewise occur in the late hours. The narrator's meeting with the duchess takes place at night.[6] The first conversation with the Cardinal and the meeting with

Marcantonio occur respectively in the late evening and in the night.[7] The Princess D'Espoli's parting from Blair is at night.[8] The secret sessions at the magician's take place at night.[9] In the villa of Horace, night is the time of convivial gathering. All decisive conversations are at night.

In Part Two the narrator is drawn into tragedy. The Duchess d'Aquilanera is the representative of an ultraconservative nobility for whom the present is an irksome annoyance and who would preserve the past with all aristocratic arrogance. Her son, who is supposed to continue this outmoded and ridiculous style of life, has early fallen into such dissipation that the plans for the aristocratic marriage are actually in difficulties. Thus the remarkable situation has arisen in which the Puritan New Englander, the man of middle-class restrictions, is destined to be the helper and healer. With a certain irony on the author's part—an irony which perhaps descends at times to facetiousness—the cure is prescribed. A mixture of long-distance running, continence, and Puritan admonitions finally leads to the collapse. In erotic confusion, the young marquis is driven to his sister, and, in an access of remorse, commits suicide.

The story that follows introduces the hopeless and humiliating love of the Princess D'Espoli for the archaeologist Blair. Here again Wilder's manner is not without a comic touch, though it is less characteristic of this chapter than of the preceding one. For the interpretation of the action the author employs the figure of Petrouchka from the Stravinsky ballet of the same name. On the evening of the farewell "Petrouchka" is danced, and Princess Alix must watch the performance without the person she loves, who by departing has given her a distinct refusal. Petrouchka becomes for the Princess the embodiment of unrequited love. The music of the ballet evokes sorrow in her, and as she goes in search of help to the magician—whose way Blair too intended to explore—she is entirely under the spell made on her by Petrouchka and the juggler.

From the question of personalities, which is a more old-fashioned—as well as primarily personal—treatment of conservative interests, Wilder proceeds in Part Four to a real concern of a member of the Cabala: the wish that the Divine Right of Kings be proclaimed as a dogma of the Church. The main character has here to assume an intensive "task of Mercury." He has to urge upon Cardinal Vaini the desire of Astrée-Luce that the Cardinal build the documentary foundations for this theory in dogma, Church law, and politics. The undertaking leads finally to a twofold destruction. The Cardinal longs for his earlier missionary activity in China. He is too sophisticated to recover real faith; all he can now really hope for is in his old work to evade otherwise certain skepticism and reach a condition of activity anaesthetized by outward missionary labors. Death on the journey spares him the attempt. Through the Cardinal, Astrée-Luce is led to an extreme skepticism that evokes malicious reactions but produces none of the fruitful beginnings that are the end result of skepticism. Astrée-Luce is for Wilder a not insignificant type. She represents faith without reflection, or before reflection, a faith that is not equal to the challenge of skepticism. This fact is not contradicted by Astrée-Luce's original concern with dogma, because this concern was not rational but mainly political and voluntarist.

A human spirit is seized with an impulsive hope, and this brings the novel's action quickly to the climax and to catastrophe. Broken, the now uncannily darkened human will hastens to its destruction. The Cabala is portrayed in the moment of its disintegration, as the new Mercury conducts it to Hades. Allusions to the downfall of Europe now become occasionally explicit: "Europe is dying. . . . All the voices of nature kept repeating: Europe is Dying." [10]

In the course of its action the Cabala represents what has become a mere farce of genuine conservatism. The Romans are no longer certain of their cause. In the new world that which is old is prized even in copy; the Romans, in contrast, are almost ashamed of possessing even genuine original. The historical turning point treated here is interpreted partly through the figure of Vergil, who is invoked by the author and the narrator. He is the key to the historical turning point in the widest sense. The words by which he is summoned are: "Oh, greatest spirit of the ancient world and prophet of the new . . . thou first Christian in Europe." [11] Wilder is here referring to the medieval European tradition which proceeded from the content of Vergil's Fourth Eclogue and claimed the latter as the harbinger of Christianity. Vergil, the last pagan and the first Christian, symbolizes here the very idea of an historical turning point. He points to the road for the new era of the 1920's. He speaks of Rome as the city of the past, and in the final conversation between him and the author the attribute "great," which has an honorific character, refers instead to New York.

Vergil invoked in this faith presupposes that the author, much as he cherishes the intellectual tradition of Rome, is not uncritical in his approach to the social structure of this old, outmoded world, which is only a shell of its former self. This social structure is the substratum in which the Cabala in Rome and its vicinity live. Naturally Wilder has not written a social novel properly so called; for that was not what he envisioned—even in *The Cabala,* this early attempt in novel writing—concerned as he was with philosophic problems of essence and problems of anthropology. An exclusive society such as the Cabala, which stands in opposition to its own time, must as a result of its retrograde structure necessarily raise the question as to the kind of social world in which it lives. This question is posed early in the novel, and Blair's derogatory term "social swells" probably reflects Wilder's own opinion.

In accord with the above characterization of this social world of the Cabala's members are the ideas regarding working and having a profession that are occasionally voiced in these circles. The Princess D'Espoli is "delighted . . . to think that their husbands did anything." [12] According to Wilder, real crisis, such as occurs in the loss of one's faith, when not accompanied by further shocks, has a comic effect on persons not involved. "The loss of one's faith is always comic to outsiders, especially when the loser is in fine health, wealth, and a fairly sound mind. The loss of any one or all of these has a sort of grandeur; Astrée-Luce should have the loss of her faith depend on one of the others. It's not a thing one loses in fine weather." [13] The groundwork for Wilder's thesis that in the question of faith personal shock is the essential element is laid in this novel, where an actual loss of faith takes place only through a profound shock and not through intellectual deliberation.

The unreal and somewhat grotesque-seeming social sphere of this novel may be said to be paralleled by the Cabala's unrealistic endeavors. Preservation and restoration are its goals; they are in bondage to the past. The archaeologist Blair calls them the moderns—they must of course seem modern to an archaeologist.

The novel alludes to various epochs of history which are connected by a common guiding sense. Cardinal Vaini knows of this. He outlines no doctrine of cultural morphology of the various phases of human history, but the books he has around him allow conclusions to be drawn. Whitehead's *Appearance and Reality,* Spengler's *Decline of the West,* Frazer's *Golden Bough,* Joyce's *Ulysses,* Proust's *Remembrance of Things Past,* and Freud's psychoanalytic works are strange reading for a prelate. On a simple level of meaning they indicate his godlessness, which the reaction to catastrophe was bound to cause in a temper still in part naïvely devout. But they also intimate that only the ancient and modern layers of history are revealed and that they could be comparable stages of two different historical cycles. But the relation of these two epochs to each other does not mean that all epochs have the same value. Functionally and morphologically the gods of antiquity are still in our midst. Their perfection is seen in the immediate, unreflecting quality of their conduct: "Godlike I never reflect; all my actions arrive of themselves. If I pause to think, I fall into error." [14]

The directness with which they act also guards them against death. Not unless and until their will is broken are they led into the state of mortality and beyond into the Kingdom of God. "All gods and heroes are by nature the enemies of Christianity—a faith trailing its aspirations and remorses and in whose presence every man is a failure. Only a broken will can enter the Kingdom of Heaven." [15]

There is an overlapping of epochs in the question of faith, but Christianity raises a fundamental question. Does the prostration of the spirit, as introduced by Christianity, not lead, with the surrender of the "cult of themselves," to a religious reality, to more than a phenomenon of cultural morphology? Vergil's place in the tradition invoked by Wilder therefore appears relatively favorable because, though he is guilty of the sin of anger, Dante is guilty of the sin of pride.[16]

In the Christian Parnassus, through which Vergil knows his way so well, and which is discussed by the main character and Vergil on *The Cabala*'s final page, Milton is held in high esteem. Erasmus debates with Plato, and Augustine joins them. But not Shakespeare: ". . . he was neither the enemy nor the advocate of grace, and being arrived in your region his whole mind may well have been consumed with anxiety as to his eternal residence." [17]

From a certain standpoint, much has been lost with the pagan deities. Because they very often represented the projections and exaggerations of human qualities, they lost these attributes when the latter were no longer believed in; they became mortal, at least they often became in part mortal. They sometimes appeared ridiculous to themselves because humans laughed at them for having lost omniscience, freedom from care, invisibility, or the power to impose a curse. But what still remained to these pagan deities, despite everything, was the stock of furnishings of a great world, in which and from which they could live in their own form, unlike the temporally delimited Christianity. To this realm of the pagan gods belonged a worldly festive mood, dominion over material things, the ability to die when it suited them, the ability to live "beyond good and evil."

Wilder, the Christian author, had had too long and too strong a contact with the culture of antiquity for him to deny its value. But this value is not the final one. Vergil, who addresses the young American as "importunate barbarian" [18] and who in reference to their conversation admonishes him to . . . "give heed to your Latin," [19] is the "prophet of the new (world)," [20] but this new world is not only that in the original Christian sense.

The main character leaves Rome for the new world. Wilder employs in this novel—as in many of his later works—a kind of parallelism in the opening and closing scenes. At the beginning of the story the author comes to Rome from America full of hope. All through his school and college years the plan of the Eternal City has hung above his desk and awakened great expectations in him. A strong

disappointment awaits him instead. He arrives in Rome at
night in a dark train, the Campagna too is shrouded in
darkness, and Rome at first receives him quite inhospitably.
Quite different is the atmosphere of his departure. The sea
offers a clear road for the voyage to the new world. The
departure is also at night, but now and again the night is lit
with stars.

It is a setting in which Vergil can be invoked. Vergil, the
escort through the ages as well as escort to the new, knows
the worth of Rome and can decide whether the author's
time there is now complete. "Master," the latter says, "I
have just spent a year in the city that was your whole life.
Am I wrong to leave it?" Vergil's answer is an affirmation of
the new in the world situation of the third decade of this
century. The new is again the great hope of man, though
now in secularized form. "Seek out some city that is young.
The secret is to make a city, not to rest in it." [21]

Despair and hope are reflected in the key words that
describe the arrival and the departure: "late"; "cold";
"darkness"; "dim"; "sigh." They are matched by the picture
of Rome: "dejected airs"; "ugly station"; "shadowy streets."
In contrast are the sense effects used in describing the
departure: "cloudless sky"; "Orion in his harness of gold";
"the stars were glittering and the water was glittering";
"pulsations of light"; "half silver and half gold." [22]

In Rome the life of the Cabala, grotesquely tortured by
ancient problems, runs its course. The problems are not
those of the new world, but this does not mean that the
latter has the right to view what is great in the old world
with bold and impudent curiosity. To impart this lesson,
Wilder introduces two secondary figures. One is a female
high school teacher from the Midwest, who has come to
Rome to verify for herself that the Forum is still there. The
other is Mr. Perkins, who with "American determina-

tion" [23] has set himself to see Rome as thoroughly and at the same time as quickly as possible, and who is not at all shy about setting foot on the tragic sites of contemporary Rome.

Perkins serves ironic literary ends in more than one respect, however. The manner of describing the death of Marcantonio, with its piling up of ridiculous European titles of nobility, satirizes the degenerate society as well. It is not out of the misguided old nor the misguided new that that for which Vergil makes himself the advocate can arise. [24]

To the old city is contrasted the new: "Seek out some city that is young." [25] New York is the new *urbs*. Vergil says very plainly that it was a great illusion to believe that the Rome in which he had lived was to last forever: ". . . I spent my whole lifetime under a great delusion—that Rome and the house of Augustus were eternal." [26] His newly won Christian conviction is that there is nothing new except Heaven. Rome is now for Vergil the embodiment of "the city" in whatever time or place, not only today in the form of New York but in earlier centuries as well. Just as Rome was not the eternal city, neither can New York be eternal, for "there will be Romes after her." [27] Under the Cabala, Rome can no longer be Rome. A backward-looking endeavor ends in the grotesque and in petrification; in terms of human lives and hopes it ends in tragedy that is by no means always dignified. A genuine *metanoia* does not follow or else does not come to an issue. In the middle chapters of the novel Wilder does not theorize a great deal; much less does he take a didactic tone. A remark he occasionally makes, that he does not wish so much to be the chronicler of the Cabala as he wishes to be the portrayer of individual human destinies that are played out within its sphere, guards him against becoming abstract and general.

The negative features of Americanism also are too ap-

parent in this novel for Wilder to be accused of an un-
thinking credulity for things American. Not that these two
Americans are unreservedly accepted by European society
either. The Spanish envoy cannot understand a country
where the worth of a person cannot be immediately recognized by his titles. Members of Roman society seem to
regard the educated American as a kind of red Indian, and it
is considered a sign of debasement when a member of this
society stoops to coaxing American couples to pay him a
visit. Yet the attempt is undertaken to make the narrator
the instrument of the healing of Marcantonio. In this novel
there is developed the theme of the polarity of the European
and the American world, especially in its New England
Puritan version. Submission and surrender to the natural is
the European and especially the southern-European way of
life, whereas the Puritan experiences the world as resistance. The natural form has deteriorated into excess, and
the Puritan must prop it up. Certainly one is no longer
thinking here of the religious ascetic background of Puritan-
ism; the intention is only to achieve the effect that a New
Englander can have upon some members of the Cabala.
The countermeasures lead to catastrophe. If, as Santayana
has deduced from New England's conditions, the world is no
longer salutary and untragic in its course, this is still less so
when it is transposed to Europe with that continent's grotesque confusion of the various elements described above.

Vergil, who knows the conditional quality of all things
Roman, ends nevertheless by calling for an intense devotion
to the new Rome of our time. It was his illusion to believe
that his Italian Rome was eternal, yet without this illusion
Rome in her greatness would not have been possible—a
truth that in Vergil's view must also apply *mutatis mutandis*
to the Rome of the new world. To be bound intensely to
worldy things must lead inevitably to a great unfolding of

culture, in whose manifestations in America under these conditions the author seems to believe.

The sight of the Mediterranean moves Vergil deeply by its renewed evocation of all earthly beauty. He inclines strongly to the world, then renounces it once and for all. Important as the genuine old world is for the best of its culture and for its perceptions of the truly human, it is also essential, in a truly decisive moment of human existence, that it be forgotten. "I cannot enter Zion until I have forgotten Rome," [28] says Vergil shortly before he leaves, never to return. The world of Zion is for him the essential world. In Zion thinking is not in riddles, and man no longer wanders about in the mists of passion.

Were Vergil not so earnest and consequential here, one would be tempted to hail him as a pragmatic of sorts who regards the *als ob* of intensity as the precondition for justifying his own existence. Vergil's goal is the intensive life of the present; to pass that life by will lead of necessity to comic and tragic complications.[29] Though scrutiny of the meaning of the past in *The Cabala* is often given a comic and ironic turn, the chapter entitled "The Dusk of the Gods" shows, on the other hand, where in the modern world the actual value of such an undertaking lies and where it does not lie.

Despite its apparently esoteric design, *The Cabala* is not literary escapism. Wilder, who is close to the great tradition, poses again and again in his subsequent novels the problem of scrutinizing the sense of past tradition. Recorded history and the historical novel offer examples enough for this. But though written with great care and discretion, they are not just historical documents translated into a literary medium, but will again and again become for Wilder instruments by which he can light his own way, a way that cannot and must not lead to missing life in the present. In *The Cabala*

Wilder has not written a period novel, nor has the way yet been fully paved for what was to be such a decisive mark of his later writing, namely, the presentation and analysis of basic existential questions of anthropology. In *The Cabala*, however, he has oriented the action to the eschatological, without allowing this to unfocus his vision for the very personal and human.

⤙ 2 ⤚

The Bridge of San Luis Rey

As a whole as well as in its individual parts *The Bridge of San Luis Rey* is closely constructed. In the interest of working out the specific statement of the problem, the work's form and its content are very much harmonized.[1] The very arrangement of the book's five chapters shows a symmetry that serves the general theme. The first and the fifth chapters set forth the decisive problem: Chapter 1 is entitled "Perhaps an Accident," Chapter 5 "Perhaps an Intention." The middle chapters are named after the persons who perished in the bridge's collapse. Chapter 2 is named after two female characters, the Marquesa de Montemayor and Pepita; Chapter 4 after two male characters, Pio and Don Jaime. The title of Chapter 3 is a kind of surprise: Esteban, who in a certain way is interchangeable with his twin brother, Manuel.

In the chapter titles, then, Wilder has featured only those characters who seem important to the theme of "Accident and Intention." They are by no means the only principal characters, nor are they all the principal characters. La Perichole and the Abbess, who form connecting links between large sections of the plot and must be numbered among the principal characters, are not mentioned in

16

the chapter titles. These two figures are, of course, not so essential to the solution of the theodicy problem in the narrower sense, that is, the one that is bound up with the plot. But they are significant for the question of the metaphysical background of life, a question that in *The Bridge of San Luis Rey* lies hidden behind the obvious problem seen by Brother Juniper.

In the foreground, outwardly emphasized, is the problem of theodicy which has arisen out of the collapse of the bridge. The sifting of the materials collected for that purpose is carried out on various levels. There are the contemporary eyewitness and earwitness reports which Brother Juniper compiles so industriously and laboriously, toiling over their interpretation. The judgment, on the other hand, is undertaken by the author. The subjects of discussion are the eighteenth century of the chronicler and the present day of the twentieth-century novelist. Our contemporary novelist has entirely avoided a careless treatment of the material. His manner of injecting his own commentary is gentle and restrained.[2] He points to events that are still to come. He does not judge, but rather leads and guides the reader through the confusion of all the phenomena to be judged. He sets forth in detail the facts previously collected by Brother Juniper for judging the theodicy problem. We learn the date of the accident, we are made precisely acquainted with the type of construction of the bridge, and we are informed about the life and attitude of the population of Lima.

These concrete details of the environment are worked into the novel—as in the eighteenth-century novels of Defoe and Swift—in order to help blur the reader's consciousness that the entire story is fiction. Wilder—whose aim in *The Bridge of San Luis Rey* is to approach with poetic means a theological and philosophical problem which comes into focus more as a question of essence than of existence—begins in the opening pages just like the author of a realistic novel, only without the latter's exhaustive narrative style.

Such a start seems to assure objectivity. In addition there is, in the person of Brother Juniper, an informant who is serious in his intent. In the reader's eyes the seriousness of course cannot be long sustained. In a manner that, while not exaggerated, certainly has more-than-mischievous overtones, Wilder lets the reader know that the treatment and solution of the theodicy problem are misplaced in the hands of Brother Juniper. This person who has ventured to examine the problem is a Franciscan, and consequently not someone on whom such a task would devolve *ex officio* as it would on a Dominican. He is moreover a man who previously failed with a similar problem, when he was about to write a study of the relation between praying for rain and rainfall.[3] In his present task, he believes that everything can be decided by a discussion of the question of good and evil.

The discussion of good and evil, and—parallel to it—reward and punishment, played a not inconsiderable role in early American intellectual history, and, in secularized form, continued to do so in later times. Good and evil, as they are released by man's actions, must accordingly—so to speak, by post-audit—be ascertainable in the life of the individual man. The quotient of such a calculation, for Brother Juniper, should reveal the meaning in man's departing this life. Brother Juniper therefore sets up his tables, which with their major headings of "Goodness," "Piety" and "Usefulness," and with ratings of zero to 10, should bring clarifying order into the seemingly contradictory life of man.[4]

But these tables are a parody, a *reductio* of Brother Juniper's primitive approach *ad absurdum*. The laboriously compiled figures merely reflect the ancient truth that what is good is not always useful and vice versa. Formulas such as "Vera N.: Goodness Zero, Piety 10, Usefulness 10" induce in the laughing reader a suspicion of difficulties with the Sixth or the Seventh Commandment. But this primitive system of judging people is not a closed chapter of the past, bound to the naïvely pious endeavor of a Spanish Franciscan in eighteenth-century Peru. Such a primitive method of evaluating human beings is still at work even in present-day America. Reflected in Brother Juniper's tables we can see the grading system of the American college. How many persons may there be today who even attempt to draw metaphysical conclusions from such a primitive procedure? Brother Juniper finally liquidated his system by tearing up his results. Are the advocates of such primitive moral inventories today willing to do the same?

The religious chronicler of eighteenth-century Peru overworks his facts a bit. He catalogues them, he makes of them a kind of system of key words. He sees man's existential plight, but without drawing from this recognition the necessary consequences. These consequences, however, the modern author helps us to arrive at. The tribulation of the human beings in *The Bridge of San Luis Rey* is defined in the very structure of the book by a remarkably strong isolation. Although the ordering hand of the author has grouped various persons together, the cohesion of the individual figures in their human origins is astonishingly small. Of the five people who lost their lives in the bridge's collapse, not one grew up in a normal parental home. Pio and Don Jaime are illegitimate, Pepita and Estaban are orphans, and the Marquesa de Montemayor is on bad terms with her parents. The second group of people—the Abbess, La Perichole and Dona Clara—are in a similar kind of isolation. Isolation is a favorite theme of Wilder's which he never relinquishes. With striking frequency one or another of his characters laments; "I am alone." [5]

The theme of situational isolation is overworked in *The Bridge of San Luis Rey* because it is so useful for erecting the theses. But this is by no means the sum of Wilder's view concerning isolation. The situation can increase isolation, but the latter is already deep-seated in human nature. The decisive words on this appear in *The Angel that Troubled the Waters:* "I am myself and no one else." [6] Brother Juniper's effort in collecting and evaluating founders in this identity isolation: "The longer he worked the more he felt that he was stumbling about among great dim intimations." [7] The consciousness of personality and thereby of the greatest possible knowledge of identity is accompanied, says Wilder, by the painful experience of solitude.

Wilder's statements concerning isolation place human imperfection strongly, indeed drastically, in the foreground. In *The Bridge of San Luis Rey* Wilder adopts positions that he will later partly qualify or abandon entirely. The family, which also later on is subjected to criticism and yet significantly embraces the life-cycle of birth and death, is characterized in *The Bridge of San Luis Rey* as organized lovelessness. [8]

Wilder develops the theme of human imperfection still further. It is not only a matter of imperfect knowing, nor is it the imperfection of humans lacking relationships to each other. Wilder inclines to the view that suffering too is an essential mark of human existence. Suffering accompanies man as a constant negative, like Original Sin for the Protestant Christian. Much of the plot of *The Bridge of San Luis Rey* is directly aimed at emphasizing this idea. The main happening—the collapse of the bridge—shows that where sorrow seems to be overcome a tragic circumstance gives rise to new sorrow, over which people can only puzzle helplessly without understanding.

The treatment of man's essential imperfection bears directly on the portrayal of death. Death and dying are discussed and portrayed in almost all of Wilder's works. In the *Bridge* it becomes central to the author's view of human existence. The chapter entitled "Perhaps an Accident" relates the death of the five people who were snatched into the depths with the bridge, and every single one of the middle chapters resolves itself into a depiction of an individual's death. Death is the incurable sickness of man. There is no effectual reasoning for him in the face of it. Nor is Wilder's the Christian conception of death as the curative process ordained by Divine Providence to lead man to immortality. For Wilder here the question of death very often narrows down to the question of when and how.

Death and suffering can only be regarded as the essentially determining factors in human life. In the realm of metaphysical questioning, this outlook does not lead us far. It could lead onward in the portrayal of the development of man as personality, with which Wilder is here of course not much concerned. He shows, however, that there is neither complete avoidance nor despair; acceptance of suffering and death is necessary to human existence. Wilder has expressed this most distinctly in *The Woman of Andros:* ". . . there is one thing greater than curing a malady, and that is accepting a malady and sharing its acceptance." [9]

Do resignation as to solving the theodicy problem and the doctrine of acceptance of suffering and death lead to complete resignation also as regards the question of knowing God? The religious problem, which in *The Cabala* arises only toward the novel's end, in the *Bridge* is often expressed or implied. The asking of the question, however, is approached by Wilder with great caution, a caution which otherwise also characterizes the book. It is not only the question of the "great perhaps" which is discussed in reference to the Marquesa de Montemayor; the "perhaps" also intrudes itself into the details of the presentation. Of Brother Juniper we read, for example: "Perhaps it was the pure air from the snows before him; perhaps it was the memory that brushed him for a moment of the poem that bade him raise his eyes to the helpful hills." [10] Of the Marquesa there is this: "She was listening to the new tide of resignation that was rising within her. Perhaps she would learn in time. . . ." [11] Or there is the Master of the University of San Martin speaking of his investigations regarding the character of a deceased person of good repute: "Nevertheless, what I said was true. This woman was an exception, perhaps an exception." [12] Seen from the standpoint of this careful kind of approach, the cautious proceeding in recognizing the person corresponds to the cautious proceeding in metaphysical cognition.

There are in the *Bridge* characters who are, so to speak, *ex officio* Christians, such as the Abbess or Brother Juniper, for whom the existence of God is never a problem. More difficult for them is recognizing the manifestation of this existence, which Wilder, speaking of Brother Juniper, sums up in Milton's words, to ". . . justify the ways of God to man." [13] When this attempt seems to have miscarried, he confesses his error before the Inquisition and sees in submission and obedience to his Order the fulfillment of his life.

The primitive Christian is the Marquesa de Montemayor, who links her belief in God to the fulfillment of her personal desires, above all to her desire that her love for her daughter in Spain be reciprocated. Birth and education had made her familiar with religion as pure faith. But the more intense she grew in her desires, the more did prayer become awake in her in the form of conjuration, and religion assumed the form of magic. Wilder's brother Amos is a follower of Bultmann's demythologizing endeavors. Both brothers are the product of rationalist American Protestantism, and Wilder in the *Bridge* shows how the Marquesa in the extremity of her desire falls doubly prey to magic: ". . . the Marquesa did not only satisfy the rites of paganism; she studied the prescriptions of Christianity as well." [14] She observes all the pagan taboos and also practices the other formulas of paganism. She seems to be a victim of the *natura maligna* that invites mockery. She turns with her wishful Christianity to the sanctuary of Santa Maria de Cluxambuqua, which is a perfect example of the superimposition of Christianity upon the forms of ancient magic religion. Even before the civilization of the Incas, violently deranged persons had loved this cliff formation, had scourged themselves there to obtain from heaven the fulfillment of their desires. Then it became for the Incas the site of magical conjuration, and finally it had served Christianity as a kind of shrine. But on this site of religious magic the Marquesa forgoes her condition that her belief in God depends on the fulfillment of her personal desires so that she may acquiesce with great submissiveness to her destiny. Here again Wilder's basic outlook becomes visible: only an existential shock can lead to faith.

In order to suggest a metaphysical foundation in his work, Wilder has assigned to nature a kind of transcendental signification. In the *Bridge* nature is not frequently in evidence, nor are there descriptions of nature for their own sake in the story. Rather, nature appears where a human being has to make decisions, or where he is forced to reflection by the decision of fate.

As Brother Juniper approaches the bridge, the sight of

the Andes at the very moment of the catastrophe is made by the author to serve to contrast the momentary tragedy with everlasting nature. Shortly before the five victims of the disaster reach their goal they behold the stars. For the Marquesa de Montemayor on the last evening of her life, the sight appears significant:

> It was almost dawn when she finished the letter. She opened the door upon her balcony and looked at the great tiers of stars that glittered above the Andes. Throughout the hours of night, though there had been few to hear it, the whole sky had been loud with the singing of these constellations. Then she took a candle into the next room and looked at Pepita. . . . "Let me live now," she whispered. "Let me begin again." [15]

The threatened state of man is here contrasted with the eternal order of nature. When Brother Juniper destroys the so-called results of his research in theodicy, he is standing in sight of the Pacific Ocean. When the Marquesa detaches herself from her pseudo-religiosity, she senses the music of the spheres. The sky is often the foil for restless man. In this regard Wilder's later works are revealing. The stars stand for that which is firmly established. They create the perspectives that give the individual his belief in the firmly established and take from him his overweening pride.

Among the natural phenomena that have symbolic character in Wilder's works are the clouds. Unlike the stars, they do not suggest a contrast but a parallel to the human condition. Just as the clouds—inevitable and significant as they may seem to the subjective view—are a transitory phenomenon of nature that is overrated in its importance, so also the psychic situation of man is only temporary and often, as a result of human exaggeration, false. There is an impressive illustration of this when the Marquesa de Monte-

mayor is separated from her daughter and thereby seemingly
loses the sense of life's meaning:

> Dona Clara sailed with most admirable composure, leaving her
> mother to gaze after the bright ship, her hand pressing now her
> heart and now her mouth. Blurred and streaked became her
> view of the serene Pacific and the enormous clouds of pearl that
> hang forever motionless above it.[16]

Wilder gives this parallel special value inasmuch as it is
not in the Marquesa's case a real existential shock. The
shock resulting from wishful thinking and that resulting
from wishful pseudo-religion are closely related. Where the
relationship to God and to the religious sphere is not
marked by a false intellectualism, it is often led astray by a
falsifying sentimentality and passionateness. The relationship, the kind of *conversio* of man toward his fellowmen is
often in the *Bridge* a kind of Index of religious feeling. Just
as passionate and sentimental persons can have no real
religious feeling, so also is this lacking in those who do not
have a genuine *conversio* toward their fellowmen.

Their love can sometimes find expression in the self-
satisfying literary form of letter-writing. Because of the great
physical distance from her daughter, letters are the Marquesa's only means of communication. Eventually she lives
entirely for these letters she writes her daughter, so that her
life, sharply reduced in its activity, seems to acquire meaning only in the writing of them. The Marquesa's participation in the proceedings of the outside world is often limited
to their usefulness as matter for her letters. This is, as a
matter of course, the only meaning for her in a visit to the
Commedia.

The love of the mother for her daughter remains one-
sided. It is a possessive love on the part of the older woman.

The daughter she idolizes owes it to her to entreat her forgiveness for the way the daughter has rejected her. The thought of a scene of pardon and reconciliation with the daughter works in her so strongly that she appears to project this wishful thinking into a forgiveness scene with the actress Perichole. She addresses the latter as "my beautiful . . . my gifted child . . . my daughter," [17] and the choice of words for the child in this case has probably more than the usual metaphorical significance.

The Marquesa de Montemayor does not take the world as it is; she wants to dominate it with the world of her own imagining. She is not entirely unconscious of this situation and wants to free herself from the "ignoble bond" of such a love.

> . . . for she knew that . . . though her love for her daughter was vast enough to include all the colors of love, it was not without a shade of tyranny: she loved her daughter not for her daughter's sake, but for her own. She longed to free herself from this ignoble bond; but the passion was too fierce to cope with. . . . She wanted her daughter for herself; she wanted to hear her say: "You are the best of all possible mothers"; she longed to hear her whisper: "Forgive me." [18]

The change, the liberation from the thought of possessing and dominating, begins in an act of resignation, of which the Marquesa becomes thoroughly conscious. The scene takes place at Cluxambuqua, and the first result is that she gives up asking things of her beloved child and of the gods as well: "Perhaps she would learn in time to permit both her daughter and her gods to govern their own affairs." [19]

The Marquesa surrenders herself to this resignation when her daughter writes her a very offensive letter. She accepts it unquestioningly, not even hoping that her daughter ask her pardon. Resignation in Wilder's writings has as its consequence the renunciation of the desire to possess and to dominate. It leads to disinterested love of one's fellowmen and to submission to God's will.

The prerequisite for disinterested love, however, is personal courage. The so often misguided religiosity of the Marquesa had its explanation in this lack of courage. It had led her to superstition and alcoholism so that she might not have to face destiny with her senses awake.

Lastly, for disinterested love there must also be grace. The Marquesa after her long delusion recognizes that readiness for grace is necessary, and that in its ubiquity it is the guarantee that love will take effect: ". . . learn at last that anywhere you may expect grace." [20]

The relationship of the Marquesa to Pepita serves to elucidate the same theme. Pepita suffers under her duties with the Marquesa de Montemayor. Only her love for the Abbess makes her endure the service of the noblewoman. The connection with the Reverend Mother and still more the possibility of seeing her gives the girl hope. Her letter to the Abbess is a beautiful monument to the timid desire and the touching submissiveness of the still childlike novice: ". . . but all this is nothing if you like me and wish me to stay with her. . . . I want to do only what you want, but if you could let me come back for a few days to the convent, but not if you do not wish it." [21]

Pepita struggles over resigning herself to the final, unreserved trust in the Abbess, but she also struggles that her love may not be demanding. The Marquesa is deeply impressed by this simplicity of love that has cast off pride and vanity, but her reaction is still possessive: ". . . she longed to command another's soul as completely as this nun was able to do." [22]

The turning point comes for the Marquesa only when

she learns that Pepita has not sent the letter because it did not seem to her trustful and courageous enough. Superficially, Pepita's letter was a kind of revolt against discipline. But it is more than that, for courage here does not mean the courage to revolt but to surrender oneself.[23]

In the character of Esteban, Wilder continues the analysis of personal *conversio,* discussing now the most strongly self-centered form of love, namely, sexual love. In the story of Manuel and Esteban he relates—or constructs—a special case that gives him the opportunity for a brief discussion of the themes that are pressing upon him. The twins build in the world a world of their own. Their strong resemblance to each other, of which they become conscious almost with a certain shame, sets them apart from the rest of the world. Their community, their togetherness, is such that they have a special language of their own which even the Cardinal, a noted linguist, cannot fathom. A decoding of this private language by a third person would mean a rupture of the twins' identity, for "This language was the symbol of their profound identity with one another. . . ."[24] This is for Wilder very significant. Language, like silence, has been lost to men as a means of *conversio.* Several times in the *Bridge,* Wilder gives vent to his feelings about this. The solitary ones do not meditate but speak audibly to themselves. Moreover, the children of this world have forgotten the art of listening: ". . . hearing little of what was said to them, . . . in dread of all appeals that might interrupt their long communion with their own desires."[25] Man's wishful thinking leads to imaginary conversations which are really only a reflection of himself. These twins know also how to remain silent, a quality they share with Captain Alvarado. They form, as Wilder says, a small nucleus in a world the rest of which has become corrupt through its forms of expression: improper speech, boasting, self-excuses, fine words.

The characters of Esteban and Manuel are by no means exaggerated. At an early age and in a natural way, they become familiar with the world of sex: ". . . both brothers had possessed women, and often, especially during their years at the waterfront; but simply, latinly." [26] This is reminiscent of Santayana's notion of the "natural" acceptance of sex among the Latin peoples. But this naïve-natural world is shattered by the separation of love and enjoyment. "He had lost that privilege of simple natures, the dissociation of love and pleasure. Pleasure was no longer as simple as eating; it was being complicated by love." [27] The power of discernment has awakened in Manuel, and the faculty of decision must come to full effect, but his imagination is captivated and his will fettered by passion. The natural harmony in the brothers' love is destroyed. It was based not on passionateness but on the ability to speak and to be silent and on the assumption that love is equal on both sides. Esteban's greatest sorrow is that this assumption is now for him erroneous: ". . . that secret from which one never quite recovers, that even in the most perfect love one person loves less profoundly than the other." [28]

When the erotic descended upon the life of Manuel, the twins' identity was destroyed. Esteban feels that Manuel's love for Perichole is irreconcilable with the brothers' love. The individuality of the two brothers has thus become manifest, and the twins' full mutual understanding which nature had bestowed on them has ceased.

Esteban and Manuel's exceptional situation has been abolished by sexual love. Of the beginning of Manuel's love for Perichole, Wilder writes: "Now was beginning that crazy loss of one's self, that neglect of everything but one's dramatic thoughts about the beloved, that feverish inner life all turning upon the Perichole. . . ." [29]

The loss of self, which Wilder otherwise regards as a

prerequisite for human salvation, is represented here as a
kind of perversion. It appears not as an attainment of a
high level of man's state of being, but as a feverish condition in which the victim strives for the possession and then
the domination of another human being. This finds a
parallel at the beginning of the novel in a brief characterization of the existence of the Marquesa de Montemayor:
"All her existence lay in the burning center of her mind." [30]
  For love of his brother Manuel sacrifices sexual love. But
both brothers succumb to the fruit they have plucked from
the Tree of Knowledge. Manuel in his confusion dies of a
comparatively minor wound, and Esteban is hurled out of
his faith and his patterns of life. Once when his brother was
still alive Esteban had proposed that they separate, in order
not to hinder the new direction Manuel's life appeared to
be taking. The actual final separation through death puts
him into a kind of delirium. He tells the Abbess that he is
Manuel. We see in this disturbance that the living wants to
be the dead, wants to be one with his brother, wants the
identity of the twins to be restored.
  The confusion into which Esteban has fallen has
brought him to the verge of suicide, which he had previously rejected because it seemed to him to contradict a
general law of nature: "Did you ever notice that animals
never kill themselves, even when they're sure to lose?" [31]
Only his decision to ship aboard Captain Alvarado's vessel
gives him the possibility of overcoming his extreme despair.
  The question which arose in the life of the Marquesa,
whether possessive and dominating love should determine
her life, took another form in the lives of the twins. They
had to gain maturity through renunciation—and through
the courage that finally made Esteban capable of losing his
life with dignity.
  In Part Four of the *Bridge* the world of the theater,

which had already occupied Wilder as a very young man, moves into the foreground. There is no detailed presentation of all its particulars, nor any surprisingly new programmatic overtures such as we know from Wilder's articles on the drama or such as we have since become accustomed to in Wilder's short plays and two great dramas. But there are references to the classical Spanish theater, and Wilder makes these in order to bring into play two figures familiar with that world, Uncle Pio and the actress Perichole.

With Uncle Pio the experienced man of the world enters the story. He is already so matured by personal experiences that he is no longer directly subject to their power, but the pleasure he has found in the world is still great enough. He does not wish to dominate human beings, but he does wish to form them. It is his wish that La Perichole become a great actress. He loves her, but without profound passion, and he respects her demand that there be distance between them.

For years on end La Perichole remains the center of his patient efforts. When her performance which he had helped to bring to a certain perfection declines, he attempts to win her over to a new enthusiasm. When her erotic connections deteriorate into sexual adventures and she finally can summon up for the Viceroy only a selfish love, Pio awaits a love experience for her that will accord with his own encounter with the world: "He divided the inhabitants of this world into two groups, into those who had loved and those who had not. It was a horrible aristocracy, apparently, for those who had no capacity for love (or rather for suffering in love) could not be said to be alive and certainly would not live again after their death. They were a kind of straw population, filling the world with their meaningless laughter and tears and chatter. . . ." [32] Those who love have suffered in a kind of sickness; suffering has matured them for the task of life. ". . . They never mistook a protracted amiability for the whole conduct of life, they never again regarded any human being, from a prince to a servant, as a mechanical object." [33]

Sexual love is for Pio primarily a transitory stage. His statements relate in part to sexual love and, in Wilder's opinion, cannot be taken totally as applying to love *per se;* nevertheless they touch in part the kernel of Wilder's views concerning *eros:* Love as a part of the divine neutralizes the material and the mechanical in life. But Uncle Pio must renounce plans that include his love for Perichole. Significantly, Wilder portrays this against the backdrop of nightfall: "It was the hour when bats fly low. . . ." [34]

Perichole's wealth and the possible greatness of her social position seem to place her at a distance from Uncle Pio. His last words are "But I am always ready"—for a self-sacrificing love.[35]

The love that fulfills itself by serving is then fulfilled in taking care of Don Jaime. Again Wilder significantly gives the time of day: when Pio begs to be given charge of Don Jaime's education, it is morning.

Wilder has set forth a series of miscarried forms of human *conversio:* primitive sexual love, exaggerated fraternal love, and one-sided mother love. In the person of Uncle Pio, the theme of love of one's work was sounded and received a partly positive interpretation. Likewise the question presents itself with the character of the Abbess. This example, however, tends to indicate that love of one's work can be disturbed by self-love, especially when—as in the Abbess' case—the love of work depends upon the thought of duration and thereby perhaps take on the flavor of an egoistic striving for immortal fame. The Abbess saw in Pepita the human being who would guarantee the continuance of her work in a later time. The collapse of the bridge, and with it the death of Pepita, take from the Abbess this somewhat selfish love. Pepita too in her *conversio* was freed from the selfish element that had become apparent in her devotion to the Abbess, though not through a tragic incident but—as in the case of the Marquesa de Montemayor —by her own free decision.

For Wilder, the self-perfecting of selfless love is the sole purpose that gives life meaning. In this sense the lives of the persons who fell with the bridge seem largely fulfilled. Any further questioning would be pointless because it would overtax the possibility of man to know as well as his capacity to know. The explanation of this idea is also served by the statements at the close of the novel regarding La Perichole, Dona Clara, and the Abbess. They too must give up their egoistic inclinations in order to arrive at the meaningful life which opens up to them in the work of the cloister. Labor is here by no means thought of as a narcotic. Its full meaningfulness becomes apparent only after the person has detached herself from the egoistic traits of her existence.

Although it may at first sight appear so, the catastrophe on the Bridge of San Luis Rey is not a proper example from the point of view of theodicy. The narrator has uncovered contradictions, and, as Chambrun has pointed out, there seems to be a certain contradiction in the fact that a Protestant writer, who would not be much drawn to it by virtue of his own religion, should have undertaken to treat the theme of theodicy. In justification of Wilder, allowance should be made for the fact that the setting of the story is in a Catholic country.

Clarification and elucidation come not through Brother Juniper but through the Abbess. She broods over how little still remains in people's memory about the departed ones. Of Esteban and Pepita no one besides herself really thinks any longer. Camila remembers only those who were closest to her, Uncle Pio and her son. Dona Clara remembers only her mother. Soon even these people, who are bound to the departed by ties of love, will be dead, and the memory of those who lost their lives when the bridge fell will cease to exist. But the love that has been freed on earth from its passions, the love that has been fortified through courage and brought to realization through grace will have had its meaning fulfilled.[36]

What is presented as significant is not so much what happens in the world as what is brought to realization as a result of human action and human resignation. Nor does it matter how lasting the thing was: "It seemed to be sufficient for Heaven that for a while in Peru a disinterested love had flowered and faded." [37]

At the end of all her meditations the Abbess is occupied with the thought of the bond that man's attainment to disinterested love creates between him and God: "But the love will have been enough; all those impulses of love return to the love that made them." [38] Love proceeds from God and finally returns to Him; earthly life is for a time endowed with it as with the power of God. It is from this angle of vision that the fact of the bridge's collapse must be viewed. It cannot receive its meaning through a computation of moral pluses and minuses, because that full, universal reality which embraces worlds is lacking in such a proceeding. With the final words of his explanation Wilder indicates this reality: "There is a land of the living and a land of the dead and the bridge is love, the only survival, the only meaning." [39]

For the person in religious life the interpretation will center on the knowledge of being led by God. Those who lost their lives when the bridge fell have returned to God, the origin and end of all love. Those who go on living have found a purification on life's earthly way, and have experienced the grace to recognize the life of that disinterested love which is given to those who are ready for it. Grace is given at the last, but he who travels the road to grace has to undergo severity and will be the target of sharp criticism. This explains why Wilder bestows a kind of pitying mockery on such figures as the Archbishop and the Viceroy. They remain in a state of ignorance and are not ready for grace.

In giving the story this design Wilder does not intend a pointed criticism of society. He probably was not even thinking of the Biblical parable of the camel and the eye of the needle. If in the design and execution of his story he had social classes at all in mind, his intention was at all events, by the inclusion of so many varied human ranks of life, to show the totally thorough quality of the principle of grace.

But it is an essential point that in the novel, together with the religious thoughts, human and humanistic thoughts are also proclaimed. This is shown by something said on the occasion of a theater performance: "We come from a world where we have known incredible standards of excellence, and we dimly remember beauties which we have not seized again; and we go back to that world." [40]

In the same passage there distinctly emerges the Platonic doctrine of *anamnesis;* here, as in the passage where God is spoken of as the source and the end of love, Plato may possibly have influenced the author. But Wilder both times has merely suggested Plato, and thus has avoided freighting the novel too heavily with ideas, of which it already had a considerable load since the introduction of the theodicy question.

Such questioning of course constantly imposed great structural problems on Wilder as a writer. We have already referred to the aesthetic inadequacies that have thereby arisen in the *Bridge:* the excessively repetitive thematic quality; the over-accentuated similarity in the characters' mental makeup, so that at times they almost run to type; and now and again—though done reservedly—the insertion of almost didactic reflections. But the theme of the selfless heart—which is what the *Bridge* is all about—keeps leading back from all intellectual speculations to man himself: "The art of literature springs from . . . a curiosity about human beings pushed to such an extreme that it resembles love." [41] The writer returns to his own domain.

⋖ 3 ⋗

The Woman of Andros

THE SETTING of this story is the Greek island of Brynos. The time is not stated and can be anywhere between the death of Pericles and the birth of Christ. The story's beginning and end make reference, in almost the same words, to the birth of Jesus: ". . . and the land that was soon to be called Holy prepared in the dark its wonderful burden." [1] And: ". . . the land that was soon to be called Holy and that even then was preparing its precious burden." [2]

Are these two sentences merely meant to fix the time of a historical story, and is the only difference between them perhaps that by the story's end one has drawn somewhat nearer to the time of the birth of Christ? Has Wilder, beginning with the esoteric society of Rome of the nineteen-twenties, and continuing with the action of *The Bridge of San Luis Rey* which is set in the eighteenth century, now taken the step into a still more remote past? Has he now, with a kind of historical novel, turned into the paths of literary escapism? Did he consciously wish to evade all the agonizing questions of his age?

A comparison of the design of the opening and the closing scene shows in both of them the grandiose natural setting of the Mediterranean. The beginning portrays nightfall with its effects of light on the western Mediterranean, just touched by the last rays of the setting sun; then the camera as it were moves back to focus on the deep darkness of Naples. After these few introductory sentences a piece of world history is evoked, and again there is the use of light effects: "Triumph had passed from Greece and wisdom from Egypt, but with the coming on of night they seemed to regain their lost honors. . . ." [3] The reader at first does not attach too much significance to this last sentence, because his attention is again drawn to optical phenomena as the story mentions a thunderstorm that day over Greece and the Nile Delta. ". . . A storm played about Sicily and its smoking mountains, but at the mouth of the Nile the water lay like a wet pavement." [4] From the optical phenomena of the Mediterranean, Wilder then shifts to the acoustic effects that mark nightfall on the island of Brynos: "For a time, the sound of the waves, briskly slapping against the wall of the little harbor, was covered by the chattering of women, by the shouts of boys, and by the crying of lambs. As the first lights appeared, the women retired; as the air was filled with the clangor of the shop fronts being put into place, the boys' voices ceased; and finally only the murmur of the men in the wineshops, playing at games with ivory counters, mingled with the sounds from the sea." [5]

With optical and acoustical effects we are made aware of this night of late antiquity, lit only by "confused starlight" and later by the "still unrisen moon." [6]

The closing lines of the novel begin—like the opening ones—with a detailed depiction of nature: "That night after many months of drought it began to rain. Slowly at first and steadily, the rain began to fall over all Greece. Great curtains of rain hung above the plains; in the mountains it fell as snow, and on the sea it printed its countless ephemeral coins upon the water." [7] The rain is first briefly shown quickening the entire landscape, then it is described in the fullness of its powerful effect on the people of Brynos: "The greater part of the inhabitants were asleep, but the relief of the long-expected rain entered into the mood of their sleeping minds. It fell upon the urns standing side by side in the shadow, and the wakeful and the sick and the dying heard the first great drops fall upon the roofs above their heads." [8] During this rainfall Pamphilus ponders anew the words of Chrysis, who wishes banishment of fear and an affirmation of Being.

In analyzing *The Bridge of San Luis Rey* we have already referred to the significance of natural phenomena to the story. In *The Woman of Andros* this appears in the natural parallels at the beginning and end, and still more plainly in the way the natural phenomena at the close are intensified as compared with the opening. In the final scene the fact that the hope for the Messiah is now closer to being fulfilled is made still more emphatic by the way the light effects vary from what they were at the story's beginning. In the opening scene the moon is "still unrisen," at the close it is shining brightly over Italy; and the stars, whose light was at the beginning "confused," at the end are beaming radiantly over the future Holy Land. In contrast to the feebly lit and increasing darkness in the opening scene there is the increased light at the end. This effect is further underlined by the transformation of the falling rhythm of the opening sentences into the ascending rhythm at the close. And finally, the narrow scenery of the beginning is enlarged at the end.

In the main body of the story there is no actually explicit reference to the eschatology of Christianity: but it cannot be assumed that the artistic pains which Wilder has taken with the story's beginning and end are merely intended to fix the time limits of the action.

Now if the Incarnation of the Son of God is *the* decisively significant fact of world history, a question naturally arises which men have asked long before Wilder: Did the people who died before the Christian era live in such a way that their lives can be interpreted as meaningful from the Christian standpoint? This question has variously disturbed and provoked the devout Middle Ages no less than it has many skeptics of the eighteenth and nineteenth centuries, and it has received a variety of answers, ranging from that based on a belief in Providence to the secularized apologia which places life before and life in the Christian Era on the same plane of ethical value.

As a disturbing factor in Wilder's Andrian woman, the question of the meaning of being plays an essential, almost decisive, role. It appears in different situations. It is the first oppressively painful feeling for youth, whom the mature person wants to help without having solved this very question for himself: "Chrysis continued . . . thinking that she was merely dealing with one of the meaningless accesses of despair that descend upon adolescence when the slow ache of existence is first apprehended by the growing mind." [9]

It takes the young person by sudden and painful surprise, but the "dim assignment of life" [10] remains the oppressing problem for all Greeks of this island world. Pamphilus, dogged by this problem repeatedly and subjecting himself to rigorous purges and fasts for his mental and spiritual elucidation, recalls Chrysis' words as she explains the spiritual situation of Greece: Lift the roof off a Greek house and you will find under it seven puzzled hearts.

The situation of the metaphysically helpless and bewildered person with which Wilder is here concerned builds up so that the entire story is the search for the one who is stronger. We see that Chrysis is the stronger as compared, above all, to Chremes but also as compared to Pamphilus, just as Pamphilus is the stronger as compared to his father. This is the search for the one who is more far-seeing and more discerning, and Wilder makes repeated allusions to those classes to whom these gifts are especially given, those of the priest and the poet.

To the poet belongs by reason of his office an unusual position. Not yet thirty years of age, he is sent by the high priests who have charge of the great Mysteries in Athens and Corinth to Brynos. The shrine of Brynos plays a great role in the old legend of Asclepius and his father Apollo.[11] The healing power and the poetic power are here deeply planted in the confused and sick life of man.

By his vow the figure of the priest has been raised above all confusion: "He had taken the vow of chastity, the vow that forever closes the mind to the matter, without wistful back-glancing and without conceding the possibility that circumstance might yet present a harmless deviation, the vow which, when profoundly compassed, fills the mind with such power that it is forever cut off from the unstable tentative sons of men." [12] The priest is no longer touched by human interests and passions, and gains the bridge to humanity only in the hour of the confessions of the sick and the confused. The priest's gift of Asclepius does not do away with grief, as we see in the description of his treatment of Pamphilus' sister, but it takes from man the confusion which had accompanied the illness.

Chrysis is the healer in another form. The slave and the courtesan do not appeal to the tastes of a later age, nor the courtesan even to some of her contemporaries. Of the young men who take part in Chrysis' symposium, one in his self-assertiveness makes a boorish allusion to her profession, for which he is adroitly rebuffed by her remark that, of all the forms of genius, goodness has the longest awkward age.

Chrysis is intolerable for the island of Brynos, for there the decisive influence still rests in a patriarchal social structure conservatively oriented to possession and acquisition. It is therefore not so much her dubious sexual status that gives rise to scandal as her uprooting of the youth from the patriarchal soil of the family. For the older women especially she represents the new metropolitan behavior as practiced in super-cosmopolitan Alexandria or in Corinth, concerning whose "Korinthiazein" St. Paul was later to write his Epistles to the Corinthians.

She is strongly drawn toward the sick and the helpless, for whom she has prepared a kind of home. Here she is the "magna mater," who cannot expect even meager thanks and is exposed to the defiant reactions of her charges, whom her absence annoys. She is a figure that Wilder is fond of portraying, witness the Abbess in *The Bridge of San Luis Rey* and, *mutatis mutandis,* the mother-figures in *Our Town* and *The Skin of Our Teeth.* The especially close relationship to *The Bridge of San Luis Rey* is further emphasized by the parallel to Captain Alvarado in the ship's captain Philocletus. This parallel extends to details. The maritime careers of the two are the same, both have lost a daughter, after which life seems just to drag on. In contrast to Alvarado, however, Philocletus loses his senses entirely, which makes him more in need of help and brings him fully within the sphere of the island of Asclepius.

Wilder's Andrian woman also turns to the socially helpless and broken, to those who in their loud and unrestrained behavior seem to be farthest removed from the Greek world. The Greek world strives to attain the serenity that the priest and—without many of those around her realizing it—also the courtesan possesses. The inhabitants of Brynos suffer under the thought that they cannot attain the serenity of the woman of Andros. They silently admire her:

"But as this calm and daydreaming figure appeared above them a hush fell upon the bargainers. This was the very deportment the Greek women lacked and sighed for. They were short and swarthy and shrill, and their incessant conversation was accompanied by the incessant play of their hands. The whole race was haunted by a passionate admiration for poise and serenity and slow motion, and now for an hour the Andrian's every move was followed by the furtive glances of the islanders, with mingled awe and hatred." [13]

The Andrian woman finds herself in a strange situation. On the one hand she is decried as new-fashioned and metropolitan, on the other hand she is the embodiment of the old Hellenism, the goal of the aspirations of the inhabitants of Brynos, who seem to have passed into an all-too-businesslike world. She has been able to revive the old institution of the courtesan's banquet in its greatness. Life no longer holds too many surprises for her, and she is able to bring man's spirit to maturity through the words of the poet and the philosopher. Chrysis takes up Plato's dictum that philosophy is really seriously supported only by the youth, who do not even philosophize especially well. But for Chrysis philosophy is not a mere thing by which to achieve fame, nor does it serve for her the purposes of personal apologia, much less does she regard it as an intellectual game.

Chrysis herself experiences a development and participates in the development of others. She is not complete as are the priest and the captain Philocletus, neither of whom, incidentally, is presented to us in dialogue form. On the island of Apollo and Asclepius she performs functions that belong to these divinities. But the island itself, in her day, is not visibly living in the age of either the gods or the heroes. At the time of the story it has become small and insignifi-

cant, "one of the least famous islands." The business activity
of the small middle-class man, especially the small merchant,
seems to govern their lives. The "thin natures" surround the
few who are wakeful and thinking.

With hardening in business and encrustation in the
family, people grow narrow in perception and in the heart.
The sense of Hellas as a community has disappeared: "In
the present age men were captains, or merchants or farmers,
but in the great age men had been first Athenians or
Greeks." [14] The young people complain, they note that the
classical poets call life heroic, half-mockingly they point out
to Chrysis that "life in a family is not in the same world as
life in Euripides." [15] At best Brynos is benumbed by the
acquisitive urge and regulated by a tradition that has
become habit. But the best of them become conscious of the
"slow misery of existence," and Pamphilus faces the hopeless situation with clear knowledge: "It seemed suddenly as
though he saw behind the contentment and the daily talk-
ativeness into the life of their hearts—empty, resigned,
pathetic and enduring." [16]

Out of this world of frustration the question arises,
"How does one live, what does one do first?" This question
is especially obvious for Pamphilus, who is not in bondage
to the pursuit of gain, nor is he so much under the power of
paternalism (which, by the way, is for Wilder one of the
principal causes of the pseudo-feudalism of our culture
today). Connected with this, however, is of necessity the
structure of the philosophy developed here, which is essentially a philosophy of life that must with a certain inevita-
bility lead to the development of the main characters.

The statement of the problem begins when Chrysis relates the story of the hero who was permitted to return to
earth—a motif that in altered form was again taken up by
Wilder in *Our Town*. The hero may return to life on one

condition: ". . . to live over again that day in all the twenty-two thousand days of his life-time that had been least eventful; but that it must be with a mind divided into two persons—the participant and the onlooker: the participant who does the deeds and says the words of so many years before, and the onlooker who foresees the end." [17]

The hero is not equal to the burden of living even an hour of such a life. He pleads for the revocation of his wish, but not because the earth has become odious to him—he falls down and kisses it at parting, just as later, in *Our Town*, Emily is to make a lovingly painful gesture—but because he has become with all intensity conscious of the unawareness and the lovelessness of the world. Men live as if not seeing at all the narrow limits of the span of their existence, and lead a life that is disconnected, as Pamphilus is forced to recognize even in the case of his own parents.

In the case of Chrysis, who is in a state of isolation, this disconnectedness has been neutralized by the courtesan's banquets and by her support of the sick and the helpless. She seems at first to be also protected by her love for Pamphilus, but she is forced to recognize that being in love, though a necessary state in the process of human development, is also a state of transition.

All the important persons in this story are subject to *conversio,* the turning to another. For Chrysis, *conversio* means a turning to the painful side of life, for Simo it is the increasing understanding of his son, for Glycerium and in part also for Pamphilus it is mutual love. *Conversio,* painful as it is for everyone, also means a further stage in development, the liberation from the ego.

For the two great ones of the story, the priest and the captain Philocletus, this fact is obvious. Chrysis must win liberation by effort. She describes herself as one who is dead, to whom negative human reactions can no longer mean anything. Considering the background of the Greek world of late antiquity, one is inclined to relate this to Stoicism, thinking of its strict demand for the serenity of *ataraxia,* especially since Chrysis herself desires the grand, serene attitude in death.[18]

The words, "she regarded herself as having died" [19] are explained later: "They lived at one remove from that self that supports the generality of men, the self that is a bundle of self-assertions, of greeds, of vanities and of easily-offended pride." [20]

Attainment of the state of divestment of the ego is described by Wilder as a series of trials. The initial ones— such as the ingratitude of her protégés—are not easy to pass. More difficult is that none of the participants in the courtesan's banquet is intellectually capable of following her, until she meets Pamphilus. But her love for Pamphilus is interrupted by the latter's adventurous surrender of himself to Glycerium.

The scene where this is revealed is—in the brevity of the description and in its gesture—a small masterpiece in the midst of the narrative. Chrysis asks Glycerium: " 'Who is it? What is his name?' 'It is Pamphilus, son of Simo.' Chrysis grew rigid in the darkness. Then she slowly put her feet back into the bed. Glycerium continued wildly. . . ." [21] It is the gesture of complete withdrawal into and upon oneself. A pause in the conversation follows, in which the inner agitation can be sensed by the seemingly matter-of-fact directive which follows it: "Will you go off to bed now and. . . ." Loneliness is expressed with particular clarity in the fact that her love for Pamphilus is not to be realized, and this effect is strengthened when illness overtakes the Andrian woman. Wilder further underscores this in the tectonic structure of the story by having the beginning of the illness, which is not in the center of the action, mark the introduction of the *peripetia*.

Through her activity with the poor and the helpless she is thoroughly familiar with suffering; she does not avoid it, as do most of the people of the island. But with the coming of her own sickness she is compelled to realize that suffering is not only a matter in which one helps others, but is an indispensable component of the structure of the world.

Wilder's story of the Andrian woman begins with the sentence, "The earth sighed as it turned in its course." These words become clear in the light of a passage from the short play, *Now the Servant's Name Was Malchus*. Against the backdrop of world space, Malchus approaches the Saviour with a petition.

OUR LORD: 'We will talk about it in a minute. Come by the window and look. Can you tell me which of those stars is mine?'

MALCHUS: 'Lord, all are yours, surely.'

OUR LORD: 'No, only one is mine, for only one bears living things upon it. And where there is no life I have no power. All the stars save one are lifeless; not even a blade of grass pushes through their powder or their flame. But one of them is so crowded with event that Heaven itself is scarcely able to attend to its needs.[22]

Seen under the Christian aspect, only one world has events of real importance. But this world is sorrow-laden; the sound of sighing emanates from it. It waits, in the pre-Christian time of the woman of Andros, for the Saviour who will also be its Redeemer from suffering. In the dual occurrence of the "sigher," the continuity of the action and the goal of the development of the cosmos and of world history become clear.

The eschatology of world history embraces also the people of the pre-Christian era. Naturally Wilder does not mean by this to say that the people of that era were in the Christian sense believers. Apart from the opening and closing allusions to the precious burden which is maturing, there is no reference in the story to Christianity. But leaving the question of Christianity and non-Christianity aside, faith *per se* is put to the test. Also in the ancients' sense of the term, the time of the woman of Andros was a time of incompleteness in faith. Anyone who was not a priest and subjected himself to the old rites of fasting did so in the desire to make himself interesting, like Pamphilus' brother, or he was looked on with astonishment by the multitude as an oddity, like Pamphilus himself.

And in the figure of Chrysis, who tries repeatedly to come to an understanding with the deity, we see questionable signs enough. She seems to have a predilection for Euripides, who was an exponent of those who were not firm in their faith. A prayer that she addresses to Apollo states: "If you still hear prayers from the lips of mortals, if our longings touch you at all, hear me now." [23]

As with all persons who are suffering greatly and hopelessly, her thoughts as the illness worsens pass over to the idea of a life after death, without arriving at any conclusion. Wilder comments: ". . . but the most exhausting of all our adventures is that journey down the long corridors of the mind to the last halls where belief is enthroned." [24] In this region there is no sense or purpose in trying to find one's way with rational considerations. Chrysis finally trusts solely in the hopes she has occasionally received by intuition: "She resigned herself to the memory of certain moments when intuition had comforted her, and she quieted her heart with Andrian cradle songs and with fragments from the tragic poets. She saved her strength to fulfill a last desire, one that may perhaps seem unworthy to persons of a later age. Her mind had been moulded by formal literature, by epics and odes, by tragedies and by heroic biography, and from this reading she had been imbued with the superstition that one should die in a noble manner, and in this high decorum even the maintenance of her beauty played a part. The only terror left in the world was the fear that she might leave it with cries of pain, with a torn mind, and with discomposed features." [25] Wilder's thorough mistrust of the rational method in the sphere of religion here again reveals itself.

With a certain necessity, the theodicy question is raised also in *The Woman of Andros*. It is not handled in the discursive or pseudo-discursive manner, as in *The Bridge of San Luis Rey*. Man's road to the praise of all things, good and bad, is that which Chrysis and also Pamphilus, after long doubts, at last attain. They consciously turn to the questionable and even dark sides of life, in order to arrive at the ripeness of full knowledge. Their road began with the compassion that is at the same time love. In the world of late antiquity, love is the fulfillment of compassion almost in the way that it should be with Christians.

Of the earthly figures, Pamphilus has the greatest compassion, and therefore Chrysis calls him "another herald from the future." She says: "Someday men will be like you." [26] By the peculiar use of the preposition *from* the course of world history is made reversible. Pamphilus is a herald from the future, from Christianity to the pre-Christian world. In his position in relation to suffering, Chrysis' estimate of Pamphilus is higher even than her estimate of herself: the future will, therefore, be determined by human beings such as him.

The meaning of suffering, of course, Chrysis is not able to see, but she hopes that in the underworld this sense will be given her: "Some day we shall understand why we suffer." Wilder has very consciously brought in here the figure of Alcestis. In the myth Alcestis is prepared to give herself to Death to save Admetus. Christ's death in man's stead has brought to Christianity eternal life and the knowledge of the way of salvation.

Chrysis has a presentiment and hope of the future as represented by Christianity. She accomplishes what Brother Juniper in *The Bridge of San Luis Rey* did not succeed in doing, a theodicy. Of course it is not a theodicy of a rational kind. The purification of love from its egoistic elements has led her to an acknowledgement and affirmation of life in its totality, and has placed her in a position to die a death not of despair but of hope.

She has gained this knowledge sooner than Pamphilus, who does not take it in right when she wishes to impart it to him. Her road and his road to knowledge of the truth run in a sense parallel, with this difference, that perceptions come sooner to Chrysis as the more mature spirit of the two, while to Pamphilus—as one living more than Chrysis under the aspect of a world-historical fulfillment—perceptions are granted that are more potent for the future.[27]

≺ 4 ≻

Heaven's My Destination

ALL OF Wilder's published works to date had had a setting
outside of America, and his American readers in particular
expected of him a book that was American in content or in
theme. In the nineteen-thirties a demand such as this was
not the affair of a narrow literary nationalism but of the
American social-minded literary criticism of the twenties
and thirties. The exponents of this criticism had leveled at
Wilder the reproach that he had given himself to literary
escapism, choosing themes that were remote from the America of the twentieth century or were at best connected with
the latter by posing a rather esoteric question, as he had
done in *The Cabala*.

For his new book Wilder chose the most afflicting epoch
of recent American history, the depression of the thirties. His
aim was not to write a period novel or a novel of social
criticism, nor even to have social criticism or social doctrine
play a role in the story.

Wilder does not minimize the critical situation of America at the beginning of the thirties, nor does he pass over in
silence the threatened state of individual human destinies.
The economic instability of the time is often considered, but

it is not made the solely deciding factor: the theme of the novel still remains "Heaven's My Destination."

This statement of the theme should not be given any great metaphysical weight. On the title page Wilder tells us that it is taken from doggerel verse which children of the Middle West were accustomed to write in their notebooks. The second epigraph is taken from *The Woman of Andros:* "Of all the forms of genius, goodness has the longest awkward age." This supplements the first quotation (for the reader familiar with Wilder's works) in that once again there is a zealously moralizing person who must conceal basic questions of existence and who by his words and deeds will show himself to be immature. The main character soon appears and makes a very distinctive first impression. He is a salesman for school books who is having great success in the Bible Belt. Only there can his ludicrously sectarian way have lasting success in business. He seems unaware of the locally conditioned nature of his occupational success. In order to be closer to his family he asks his firm to give him other states as his sales territory. The firm's directors, who know him better than he does himself, reject his request.

There is an old model for this presentation of the life of the modern salesman. It is the idea of a journey, a business trip which is also missionary in purpose. One thinks of a modern burlesque of the *Pilgrim's Progress* that might be made of this novel. Wilder would of course not be the first in the history of American literature to try such an experiment. Hawthorne had already attempted it in "The Celestial Railroad."

What we see here is an already existing literary model and not a modern work that in content is closely parallel to an earlier one. The journey is not directly to a visible celestial city. The chapter divisions make clear what the nature of the journey is. An action that occurs midway divides the thirteen chapters into two parts. At the midway point a severe crisis threatens; it is removed, and the plot can resume its course. In the thirteenth chapter a crisis once again threatens, and resolves itself in further wanderings as the main character "continued on his journey." The forward movement can be described as an upward spiral of constant repetition. With Brush's temperament, there can be no final attainment of the goal.

By his nature a religious person can certainly not always attain his goal, but if his strivings toward it are to appear meaningful despite the repulses suffered in the valleys of shadow in both the *Pilgrim's Progress* and *Heaven's My Destination*—witness the drunken scene and the bordello scene in the latter—these strivings must not give the impression of being an almost infinitely repetitious and mechanical design.

This design, as realized by Wilder, is that the moralizing religious man George Brush lives on abstractions. He derives these mostly by making excerpts from authors, or—as in the case of his use of Tolstoy—using such excerpts ready-made in booklet form. These he zealously urges upon his contemporaries as a moral rule of life. In this way he does not grasp the reality of his fellowmen. In blind "uplifting," the proselytizer's own ego inevitably fails to arrive at any real self-knowledge. The result is failure and the now-habitual new beginning.

The word most used by Brush in his moral crusades is "theories." In the field of literature he derives his moral theories especially from Gandhi, whose resistance to British rule brought him wide fame in the nineteen-twenties, but whose life became familiar to the American public also through widely distributed translations of his works.

In the course of the plot of *Heaven's My Destination*, Gandhi's doctrine of voluntary poverty is for the first time put into action. When Brush withdraws his money from the bank he wants to leave the bank the accrued interest on his deposit, because he does not believe in interest, in capital that works for him. Here the idea of voluntary poverty is shaped up for personal ends, and becomes a theory that, in a situation such as existed in 1930, must lead to an increased run on the banks.

Brush is himself a convert, as we learn in connection with his story of the girl preacher who kept herself going by means of drugs. As a missionary to others he has organized his own theories and added a few from his reading of Gandhi. Toward the end of the book he tells us: "Then the next important thing in my life was when I began to read about Gandhi. I got hold of the life that he wrote of himself and that gave me a lot of ideas." [1]

His simplified conception of Christianity and of Gandhi's life determines his view of the nature of a bank. Leaving out of consideration all possibly complicating factors, he sees the bank as an institution which owes its origin solely to human fear.

Brush's thesis is that banks are founded on people's fear and in turn generate fear in them.[2] The book literally swarms with theories. Another of Brush's favorite theories is that a singing voice is a gift of heaven and therefore to be enjoyed free of charge, a conviction which he puts into practice repeatedly. In addition there is his theory that—as he puts it—the world is full of wonderful people,[3] a view which leads him again and again into difficulties with people. These theories show how immature Brush is. At the end of the book there are still some theories circulating in his head and they will never cease to ferment in him.[4]

Especially interesting is his theory of sickness, about which the religious crank must necessarily have a theory of his own. In his view it is an outgrowth of man's lack of courage: "Sometimes I think I may get so discouraged that I might fall sick—or worse. Because that's all sickness is: discouragement. That's one of my theories, too. I have a theory that all sickness comes from having lost hope about something." [5] The history of the depression years was especially full of similar theories. America offered a very fertile soil for such ideas, for one of the two great religions founded there since the beginning of the last century is based very strongly on, among other things, a religious view of sickness.

Gandhi's personal life and the thoughts concerning the effects of fear inevitably awakened in Brush reflections on the doctrine of non-resistance. This finds expression in Brush's simple assertion in argument that he is a radical pacifist who, to be thoroughly true to his way of thought and action, must swallow personal wrong done to him without defending himself or striking back.[6] He repeats this assertion before the judge with reference to a possible attack in war. The monomaniac, inclined by nature to simplification, has also seized upon Gandhi's word *ahimsa* [7] and has it always ready to hand for "clarifying" all situations involving the use of force. From this comes what he calls his "theory about thieves and robbers." [8] What this adds up to is that theft and robbery would be soon eliminated from our society without those forcible measures which society usually takes against them. This leads in the course of the story to grotesque situations such as the one in Mrs. Efrim's store, where the meeting of the primitive disciple of Gandhi with the petitbourgeois profit motive of the shopkeeper shows in an inevitably droll light the questionable character of pseudo-Gandhiism.

Brush's imitation of Gandhi makes it easy for Wilder to develop other grotesque situations in the book. The combatting of alcohol and tobacco consumption enables the author to lead Brush into many situations where owing to his own abstinence he can display an overweening superiority, and divert the violent conflicts that then threaten. Gandhi's fasting exercises also appear, so as to complete the picture of the comic imitation of the great Indian.

When it comes to exercises in silence, it is less easy for Brush to avoid trouble. This touches the immediate communication with his environment, and cannot only lead to grotesque scenes, but also—aided by an evil enterprise of his enemies—brings him into court. His sectarianism and compulsive adoption of Gandhi had already gotten Brush into difficulties. His desire to give life an organized character, even where such organization seemed somewhat appropriate, had already begun when he was in college. As in *The Bridge of San Luis Rey*, Wilder also takes the opportunity here to testify to the malfunctioning of the American college in these questions. In college Brush had taken a course in religious disputation with unbelievers, which in its manner and design is an example of clumsy inquiry that is bound to provoke the other party to either laughter or annoyance.[9]

Brush did not give up his desire for a planned and thoroughly organized world after leaving college. The time span of the novel is one year, from his twenty-third to his twenty-fourth birthday—a good choice for presenting a person's life plans. We see Brush as he draws up his planned obligations for the coming year, including data regarding his ethical state: "In one hand he held a rought draft of his resolutions for the year, along with a list of his virtues and faults."[10]

The ethical plans lead to new vexations. In a quarrel with one of the people whom he irritates, Brush is characterized as the "perfectly logical man." This at first seems to please him, since his career to date had given him certain doubts of his intelligence. Among the disappointments of his student years was the fact that he was never admitted into one of the big fraternities nor into the college's literary society. In literature he had certain aspirations. His teacher had called *King Lear* the greatest work of English literature, an opinion shared by that fountainhead of his knowledge, the Encyclopaedia Britannica. But despite much reading of the play he still can find nothing in *Lear*. He therefore memorizes it in full.

The "perfectly logical" quality is to prove to be a negative one, and in a manner that Brush in his somewhat exaggerated self-confidence cannot at first understand. It is that he is the perfectly logical man who undertakes to carry out an abstract principle to the bitter end, and who thereby of necessity discredits that principle.

Brush is regarded as hopelessly "different." Direct charges cannot be sustained against him, but people can reject his obstinate way of being different. Mrs. Efrim, who is so gravely injured by Brush's foolishness, finally testifies before the judge at the hearing: ". . . I have no charges to make against that young man. I guess he is different from the rest of us, that's all." [11]

Brush's great difficulty is in the frequency with which he encounters the so-called normal, especially in its excessive forms: in drunkenness, unbridled sexuality, excessive use of nicotine, in its basic approach to the world as well as in its amazing thoughtlessness. His conversion has altered him. He cannot leave the world as it is. He wants to convert people, but the effect he achieves is that of "the fool in Christ." This fool in Christ is not utterly remote from the world. He is after all a modern American salesman, who is even successful in business matters within the limits of his small sphere, who in the depression is not laid off but even manages to increase his income. But even in his success can be seen something of his foolishness. His reports to the home office are a source of amusement to his superiors. One could almost say that whenever his life seems headed for success, it is not long before his foolishness also appears at its maximum, throwing everything again into question.

Not that Wilder portrays George Brush as a man habitually in opposition. His great helpfulness makes him most welcome to one group of people. In the depression he can be depended upon for help, and at Camp David he comes at once to the aid of the man who has failed. American literary critics have debated the question of whether Brush is a satiric character. Wilder has denied this, and said that Brush is portrayed with simple realism, not satire. This of course does not mean that the portrayal would not be satiric in its effect on the religious sectarian enthusiasts of this time.

Brush recurrently has normal and seemingly normal impulses in relation to his fellow human beings. Women do not reject him right away. True, the aim of his that runs like a thread through the entire story—his search for the missing Roberta in order to marry her and found an American home—seems likely to run into difficulties. But the biology student Jessie is responsive—until he comes out again with his foolish ideas and what is for him the big question that he is forever putting to people, namely, what is her attitude toward fundamentalism. He also could have married Roberta's sister, if he had not blocked the way to a normal marriage with his ridiculous notions about restitution.

Finally, Brush has neither a friend nor a companion on his wanderings, excepting one, Father Pasziewski, whom he has never actually seen. Thus he is an invisible companion who cannot help Brush in the world. In any case, the priest too has failed to establish rapport with the world. He has not succeeded with people. The juvenile products of his education are failures. But the dying priest's farewell gift to George Brush stirs the latter finally to resume his pilgrimage: zealous and senseless. This whole situation is recognized most effectively for what it is by a clergyman whom Brush had revered in his college years, when he tells Brush frankly what he sees that zeal has done to him: "He said: 'You've got a closed mind, Brush, an obstinate closed mind. It's not worth wasting time on you,' he said. 'I wash my hands of you,' he said, 'you'll never get anywhere.' " [12] With the words "closed mind" the author has the clergyman complete the judgment of Brush made by the atheist, that he is "the perfectly logical man."

Brush, who has gone forth into the world with missionary intent, demands too much and has too little to offer in return. He seems to be a saint, but he has by no means all the qualities of a saint, who in confessing all his weaknesses also lays down all his weapons of argument. A number of very distressing things in Brush's past are not revealed by his confession but must be brought out by questioning. Considered purely from the standpoint of novelist technique, much of this would appear to be merely the author's use of flashback. But considered in relation to Brush's character, these things indicate certain unintegrated elements of personality.

As a result of the questioning we learn what happened in Roberta's father's barn. Brush also becomes suspect in the eyes of the reader in that, even when he is telling things about himself of his own free will, he does not tell the whole truth in all its details until someone puts the specific question to him. An example of this is the following dialogue: " '. . . She was sitting in a sort of dressing room and she was sort of moaning—' 'Did you say moaning?' 'Yes, moaning and groaning. And an older woman was standing over her, sticking a hypodermic syringe into her arm.' " [13]

The not-entirely-saintly-seeming Brush gets into other difficulties which are also not readily harmonized with saintliness. Without being entirely of the world, he is nonetheless too much in the world. America has always been rich in this mundane type of saint. To this category belonged many of the American "men of good hope," in Brush's own lifetime, for example, Upton Sinclair. But these mundane saints had it easier than Brush inasmuch as they were mostly without any metaphysical foundation and, consequently, neither vulnerable to contradiction nor exposed in their imperfection.

In their missionary activity they spoke a more intelligible language than George Brush. They were rejected, sometimes ridiculed, and occasionally even persecuted— because people out in the world understood them all too well. Brush's language ultimately remains unintelligible. He cannot learn his "territory's" mode of expression. Thus there remains a strange contradictoriness in this novel, which consists—and by its nature must consist—almost entirely of dialogue, but in which all the talk never reaches the point of real conversation.

Brush's failure leads to his illness. His doctrines seem to be fulfilled in this part of the novel, for the illness is brought about by disobedience, by the powerful unresolved confusion of things in him.

Crises succeed each other periodically in Brush's life. The first crisis at the end of the book's first part is followed at the end of the second by a crisis that is nearly mortal. Brush finds his way out of it by means of the simple present he receives from a brother in spirit. But does this renewed finding of the way out have any other meaning than the repetition of awkward missionary activity which cannot lead to any goal? By his words as well as by his silence Brush will again be a source of irritation to people, because he possesses perfect knowledge and therefore will not make a movement toward gaining understanding.

Wilder means to give a lasting expression to this at the beginning of the second part of the novel, by confronting Brush with a reflection of himself. While he is riding in a railroad car, another religious sectarian approaches and harasses him.

That Brush has not changed is underscored in the novel's structure by the many repetitions in language and theme. Elsewhere in the novel Wilder employs repetitions with slight nuances, but here the repetitions are intentionally wearying and constant; where they appear in another form, it is with a view to lending variety to the narrative rather than to imparting any significant nuance to the substance.

⤟5⤞

The Ides of March

WILDER became more experimental in his use of the novel form with *The Ides of March,* a work which is difficult to classify under any of the traditional types of the novel. In content it belongs to the category of historical novel, but its real form is hard to define. One is tempted to call it a novel in letter form or some variant thereof. The extracts from diaries and agents' reports, the samples from the Roman poets and prose writers make up such a varied mosaic that a more suitable term for this work would probably be "pseudo-factual report in novel form."

The experiment we see in this novel covers not only the arrangement of the so-called facts, but also their dating and placement within the novel. Most of the "documents" used by Wilder bear an exact date; a few look back on the events from a later time. One of these latter is the report of Asinius Pollio to Vergil and Horace.[1] Another is the extract from the notebooks of Pliny the Younger [2]—written about one hundred years after Caesar's violent death—which relates a legend that a religious community devoted to the cult of the Mysteries, in order to assure the permanence of Rome, robbed and mutilated Caesar's corpse and buried the fragments separately in different parts of the city. The others are the inscription on the steadfastness and reticence of Portia,[3] and Suetonius' account of the assassination of Caesar, written seventy-five years after the latter's death. These four items, comprising in all only a few pages of the novel, are meant to show how Caesar later passed into history and legend and to extend the story's documentary quality beyond the limits of the time in which the action takes place.

The immediately contemporary "documents" are arranged in the novel's four books in a distinctive order. The earliest date of the documents in Book One is September 1, 45 B.C. The action of the First Book ends with the attempted assassination of Caesar on September 30, 45, while he was on his way to a dinner at the home of Clodia Pulcher. The Second Book includes the time span of the First, but begins earlier, on August 17, 45, and ends on October 27 of the same year. Wilder employs a similar technique in Book Three, the action of which extends from August 9 to October 27, 45—and in Book Four, which covers the period from August 8, 45 to March 15, 44. What is the author's purpose in this? Is it simply to achieve a longer point of view, or does this "overlapping" technique secure an effect of surprise or irony? The dramatic effect achieved by the attempted assassination is further advanced by the climaxes in which the succeeding Books end. The Second Book culminates in the reception given by Cleopatra, which marks the end of Caesar's relationship to her, and which is also the day of Catullus' death. The Third Book ends with the profanation of the Mysteries of the Good Goddess by the brother and sister Claudius and Clodia Pulcher. At the end of the Fourth Book, Caesar is assassinated. Central to all four Books is Caesar, who is the focal point of all the characters' thoughts and actions. In their relationship to him they yield to the historical action, but reveal at the same time much of their inner selves, and thus incorporate the tasks and questions that are identified with them.

The problems of the last years of the Roman Republic become distinct in the First Book as Clodia Pulcher moves very much to the foreground, with her destroying love for Catullus and her joint conspiratorial efforts with her brother in planning the Dictator's assassination. Caesar seems to be not without blame for Clodia's destructive talent, for she traces the responsibility for her deeds to his behavior toward her in the past.

In the Second Book two couples take the central position: Clodia Pulcher and Catullus, and Caesar and Cleopatra. Clodia Pulcher's destruction reaches one of its peaks: she is guilty of the death of Catullus, and she effects the destruction of the human relationship of Caesar to Cleopatra. The Third Book carries the destructive effect of Clodia from the human ethical sphere into the religious sphere, by the long-planned and now executed profanation of the Mysteries. Here Caesar's journal of letters to Lucius Mamilius Turrinus is an especially rich "source": the entries in the first two Books of the novel are now matched by five more entries with several contemplative enclosures.

The Fourth Book brings the catastrophe as Brutus actively intervenes. In its structure it is not unlike Book One. Brutus too, by reason of his possible relationship to Caesar, stands in close human connection to him. Like Clodia Pulcher, he represents the younger generation, although in contrast to Clodia's revolutionary strivings Brutus represents the young generation of conservatism.

The conservative and the revolutionary elements play a role in the design of the book in other ways also. One of the group of conservatives is Julia Marcia, who is related to Caesar on his mother's side, and who in a certain contrast to

Clodia is at the same time the embodiment of old age. The conservatives include, above all, Cicero, who—possibly in a continuance of older dramatic creations—is the figure of the discontented conservative. Wilder makes him the subjective, careworn chronicler of the time, who would like to take part in Caesar's overthrow but is prevented by his own timidity, thus becoming a natural victim of mockery and ridicule.

Cornelius Nepos may be regarded as a counterpoise to Cicero. He too has the function of chronicler, but performs it objectively.

The transitional character of the age is such that the perversions of Clodia Pulcher, though personal at their root, contribute greatly to the age's disintegration. Catullus, who according to this novel is the strongest embodiment of this dissolution, feels himself bound in the closest way to the current of the age. Cicero terms Catullus' poetry as opening the door wide to the no-longer-comprehensible,[4] as being neither Roman nor Greek, as the dissolution of the written Latin language with the possible splitting of the poetic ego. To the conservative Roman of the last years of the Roman Republic, all this meant a barbarism that was dissolving all the ancient forms.

With this the fact is distinctly emphasized that Caesar's opponents are not united under any single banner. But Caesar himself is also uncertain. He is regarded as the man of action: "Caesar has cultivated this immediacy in everything that he does. He seeks to eliminate any intermediary stage between impulse and execution."[5] But he recognizes the dubious nature of the time, and, through reflection, is definitely receptive to that which is new. Moreover, the recent marriage to Calpurnia seems to be for him the beginning of a new phase of life.

Amid the turbulence of the age, Caesar's solitude increases more and more. Undoubtedly this condition has been his at a relatively early date, owing to the positions he held in the army and the state. Caesar's skeptical attitude becomes at once apparent in the first document, in which he gives his opinion regarding the reports of the College of Augurs. "I have inherited this burden of superstition and nonsense. I govern innumerable men but must acknowledge that I am governed by birds and thunderclaps." [6] To the active man, the College of Augurs is not only an hindrance in the affairs of state and in the conduct of war; it is also an intellectual vexation. It creates a class, "from the street sweepers to the consuls," who gain a vague sense of confidence where there really can be none. Paradoxically they generate a fear which paralyzes equally action and thought. The Roman citizens' primary task—that of creating, moment by moment, their own Rome—is thereby rendered impossible.

Reflecting in the night hours, Caesar tries to imagine what would happen if he abolished superstition and closed all temples except those of Capitoline Jove, thus introducing monotheism into the Roman world. But purging the religious world of its polytheism is unable to satisfy Caesar's penetrating intellect. He goes back to Homer's ancient idea that God pours out from his urns his good and evil gifts. But this does not fill the world entirely; there remains reserved to our knowledge a field of circumstance on which divinity exerts no influence. The pious ones do not realize this, and Caesar goes so far as to declare that their lack of consequential perception is really an insult to their God. [7]

In the realm of religion, natural phenomena have assumed the character of hints and portents, and this has led to the fatal manifestations of superstition. Natural phenomena must be returned to their proper area: ". . . put the birds back into the world of birds, thunder back into the phenomenon of the atmosphere . . . ," and divinity itself back into the realm of children's imagination.[8] Though he regards exotic cults such as those of Isis and Osiris as attractive to the eye, to the intellectual their content is "all nonsense," something for porters and servant girls.[9] In his irritation over the way that superstition hinders the affairs of state, Caesar finally drafts an edict ordering the closing of the temples and the marriage of the Vestal Virgins. He is spurred in this by the happy feeling of honesty: "When have I been happier? What pleasures are greater than those of honesty?"[10] But he destroys the edict. In an access of radical sentiment the cult of Jove is abolished and Jove himself declared nonexistent. But this document too is finally destroyed. Why?

Caesar is not prompted by Cicero's political maxim that the absence of a state religion would leave the field open to superstition in clandestine and perverted forms. Nor is he influenced by fear that such radical measures would destroy the social order. The possible repercussions do not at all deter him from these radical measures. It is probably the ultimate uncertainty that prevents Caesar: ". . . It was something in and of myself. In myself I was not certain that I was certain."[11]

He believes himself completely certain that there is no mind behind our existence. Only then does man's role seem to possess the great tragic dignity: "How terrifying and glorious the role of man if, indeed, without guidance and without consolation he must create from his own vitals the meaning for his existence and write the rules whereby he lives."[12]

The truth of such a perception must lend a person its power and strength.

It is not fear, anxiety, or cowardice that holds Caesar back from total negation in religion. He is not altogether certain about the world's being divested of myth, and must

therefore see at once that the smallest exception to this
divestment would have, as its inevitable consequence, not a
partial but a total reversion to type in religion: the doctrine
of the existence of the gods, the immortality of the soul and
the ethical sphere—which in turn is linked to the religious
—and the view that we are rewarded and punished for our
deeds.

Though Caesar cannot banish the metaphysical element
from his views, he seeks to find in his own mind the areas
where premonitory awe still sway him. He sees it as a force
in the *eros,* in poetry, in the presentiment of a higher knowledge or higher happiness, and in the awareness that his life
and his services to Rome have been shaped by a power beyond himself.[13]—In this connection Caesar again reverts to
the subject of his immediacy of action and his habit of never
reflecting beforehand. He considers it very possible that the
gods, out of love for Rome, direct his swift efficacy by means
of some daemonic being. In later letters he again takes up
the religious symbolism. He writes to Pompeia of the Egyptian ideas and practices concerning the life and migration of
souls, and he remarks that the souls of the Romans are
anchored in the present life, so that the "washing of one's
soul" and the "passing from one stage of being to the next"
mean nothing more than Roman duties, friendships, and
sufferings if any.[14] Thus it is also understandable that he is
active in reforms of the Mysteries of the Good Goddess and
writes to the Superior of the College of Vestal Virgins that
he too is of the view that the Mysteries "held the world together from falling into chaos," [15] indeed that parts of them
could maintain the power of Rome. But, he continues, one
should also bear in mind that it is a law of life that everything grows and changes, that the dead husks of things are
shed and new and more beautiful things emerge. Thus it
should be with the religious rites also.

In the age of religious syncretism in which he lives, Caesar has endeavored to obtain an idea of the equivalents of his gods. It is easy for him to recognize that in Gaul a fusion has taken place between the god of the oak tree and of storms (Wotan) on the one hand and Jove on the other. In the eastern regions of the Empire, the temples of Venus, Caesar's ancestress, are the same as those of Astarte and Astaroth. If man's descent from Jove is regarded as universally valid, then the fusion of religions must of necessity lead to a brotherhood of man, a positive factor to which Caesar wishes that his successors would also direct their careful attention.[16] These perceptions are a structural element in the plot of the novel inasmuch as Cleopatra draws from them conclusions which she intends to bring into play with reference to her position in Rome. Caesar, to whom the Queen's theories of her divine origin appear ridiculous, must be very careful. He does not wish to admit her to the Mysteries of the Good Goddess on the grounds of the similarity or equivalence of the gods. He wishes to admit her only to the first part of the Mysteries, and only on the ground that the goddess is the patroness of all women. But despite his efforts in this to bolster and preserve the prestige of Rome, he must concede that a close connection between the Egyptian and the Roman religion exists in this very matter of the Mysteries of the Good Goddess, in which the coiffure of the Roman women is very similar to that of the Eygptian women. ". . . Who can explain the symbols, the influences, and the expressions of that universal mixture of joy and terror which is religion?" [17] writes Caesar, half in astonishment and half in despair, to Lucius Mamilius Turrinus in the late summer of 45.

The appearance and the status of Cleopatra have made the question of religion again, from another side, the topic of discussion. The many titles at the beginning of Cleopatra's correspondence serve not only the author's aim of creating an illusion of historical authenticity, but also serve to draw the reader's attention to the problem of Cleopatra's claim to divine origin. Wilder here is out for some mischievous fun, for, besides Caesar's joking comments on this question, there are also droll and grotesque scenes that are undoubtedly designed to take away the tone of pedantry from the treatment of the question of the Queen's divine origins.

Caesar himself is threatened with deification and knows it full well. In one's early years, he writes to Lucius Mamilius Turrinus, one had the feeling of being equipped with unusual powers, and out of this feeling grows a large degree of self-confidence and also over-confidence. To this Caesar ascribes the words that he is supposed to have said to a ship captain: "Have no fear; Caesar is your passenger." [18] Measuring this against the experiences of his personal life, Caesar must now concede that he was presumptuous and that he really is exposed to the bitter experiences of fate in the same way as everyone else. Caesar does not think of exploiting this sort of godlike feeling politically. He writes: "Nothing seems to me to be more dangerous—not only for us rulers, but for those who gaze upon us with varying degrees of adoration—than this ascription of divine attributes." [19]

He now resolves also to send no more gifts to various localities, because he has heard that these are made into shrines to which people make pilgrimages in search of healing and help.

In explanation of the deification of great personalities, Caesar again has his own theory ready to hand: there is an inclination to ascribe to highly placed and highly gifted persons a more-than-human nature. In Caesar's opinion, the gods and demi-gods are mere ancestors who were finally deified by posterity's reverence for their great qualities. Thinking pragmatically, Caesar further remarks that this conception of the gods had pedagogic significance for youth in that it widened their horizons and provided a sanction of good morals and the institution of the state. The decisive step in the process of deification is the interruption of the idea of *human-ness*, thus barring the idea of the expansion of that quality.

Reflecting on the nature of religion, Caesar believes that he discerns that the partial elimination of the reasonable view leads to religious and pseudo-religious manifestations. Being officially occupied with a certain sphere of life leads more or less necessarily to its rationalization and, thereby, to excluding the assumption that there are metaphysical influences. Caesar gives the example that a townswoman asks for good weather for an outing in the country, but that his own aunt, who is the owner of an estate, would not do this. She does not believe that the gods can influence the weather; she is much more convinced that the gods exert a considerable influence on Rome's destiny and that they have taken Caesar under their special protection.—Cicero does not believe that the gods would let Rome perish. He is also of the opinion that in the Catiline affair the gods may not share his honorary title of "pater patriae." Cicero is of the view, however, that the gods have implanted in man the idea of justice. Catullus, on the other hand, believes that the idea of justice originated in disputes over property and the boundaries between land holdings. In love, of course— however ignominious its manifestation—Catullus believes he discerns the workings of the divine.—For Cleopatra love is only a pleasant diversion. The most compelling feeling for her is her attraction to her children. Divinity, for her, lies in one's own energy and strength of will.

Caesar has prefaced these views with a brief semantic

consideration of the concepts of "God" and "divinity." He admits that he once believed in each of the meanings exemplified above, and that by casting them off he gained a feeling of liberation and increased strength. But precisely in this way, he gives a distinct prospect and hope for recognition of the metaphysical element: "I feel that if I can rid myself of the wrong ones, I shall be coming closer to the right one." [20]

In September 45 chain letters calling for Caesar's assassination are discovered. Caesar gives Lucius Mamilius Turrinus word of this, engaging at the same time in reflections as to what functions are intended for such a murderer by the metaphysical powers. He proceeds from the premise that the people had called him "destiny's favorite." If the gods exist, they must have placed every outstanding man where he is. A murderer, when he confronts such a man, has his assigned function to fulfill. Caesar believes that his own assassination could, in certain circumstances, help to illuminate the ancient problem of "de natura deorum," for such an assassination would of necessity disclose the metaphysical-historical meaning.

Soon, however, doubts are stirring again in Caesar's mind. If the assassination were a matter of chance after all, if, for example, a madman committed the deed? In that case the gods' behavior would be all the more enigmatic: "The Gods hide themselves even in their choice of instrument. We are all at the mercy of a falling tile. We are left with the picture of Jupiter going about dislodging tiles which fall upon a lemonade vendor or upon Caesar. The jury that condemned Socrates to death were not august instruments; nor were the eagle and the tortoise that slew Aeschylus. It is probable that my last moment of consciousness will be filled with the last of many confirmations that the affairs of the world proceed with that senselessness with which a stream carries leaves upon its tide." [21]

In the end it is not a metaphysical discovery that Caesar is granted at his assassination, but at most the surprising discovery in political ethics, that he is assassinated not out of envy but out of the strange hatred on the part of a man who sees in him the enemy of Rome.

In his next-to-last letter to Lucius Mamilius Turrinus, written presumably in March of 44, Caesar, consoling himself in his metaphysical struggles, writes that the ultimate intellectual freedom is preserved and guaranteed by the fact that—in contrast to all things physical—there are no limits set to the spirit where good or evil are concerned. Recognition of this secret prevents him from making summary judgments on questions of human existence, and causes him to maintain the hope of final knowledge. "Where there is an unknowable there is a promise." [22]

This leads us back to the epigraph at the beginning of *The Ides of March,* a passage from *Faust* that Wilder gives first in the original German:

> Das Schaudern ist der Menschheit bestes Teil;
> Wie auch die Welt ihm das Gefühl verteure. . . .

Wilder's translation follows:

> The shudder of awe is humanity's highest faculty,
> Even though this world is forever altering its values. . . .

To this Wilder adds the following gloss:

"Out of man's recognition in fear and awe that there is an Unknowable comes all that is best in the exploration of his mind,—even though that recognition is often misled into superstition, enslavement, and overconfidence." [23]

Wilder's interpretation of the passage from Goethe is without question wrong. The two lines have been isolated from their context, which reads as follows:

> Doch im Erstarren such ich nicht mein Heil,
> Das Schaudern ist der Menschheit bestes Teil;
> Wie auch die Welt ihm das Gefühl verteure,
> Ergriffen, fühlt er tief das Ungeheure.[24]

> (I do not seek my salvation in rigidity,
> the shudder of awe is the best part of man; whatever
> the world impose as penalty, he is gripped and senses
> deeply the Immense.)

Wilder has not recognized the passage's syntactical context. His placing the "shudder" and the "altering values" in opposition to each other accords better with Wilder's own psychology of religion than it does with Goethe's intention.

In his analysis of the poetic, Wilder seeks to illuminate two basic problems. The first is the problem of freedom, which in the political sphere was very restricted in 45 and 44 B.C., and which even in the theoretical field of knowledge had gotten into ever narrower straits. Caesar calls the poets "sovereign beings." [25] They can still encompass the whole of life in their view and bring the internal and the external into mutual harmony.

Cicero, in his letter to Atticus of September 26, 45, takes up the political factor: "We have become slaves, but even a slave can sing" is the tenor of his statements.[26] Reversing the procedure of Odysseus, he has not stopped his ears against the song of the Sirens, but gives his attention to the Muses in order not to hear the death rattle of the Republic.

In this hour of history, poetry finds its greatest embodiment in Catullus, who with Lucretius has helped to make

Latin poetry in some degree the peer of the Greek. Caesar is deeply impressed by Catullus' poetic gift, as is also the actress Cytheris. But again Catullus is characteristic of the transitional nature of the age.

It is not only Cicero's grumbling that limits the estimation of Catullus as a poet. The Roman Empire had experienced such an expansion that even in intellectual affairs its outer regions were able to make their forms of expression effective. People in Rome even recoiled somewhat from the northern provincialism of Catullus. Cicero in particular finds poetry like that of Catullus positively improper. He resists it because it has not sufficiently transformed the raw experience into poetry. Such poetry as this, he feels, cannot be called Roman; formerly poetry had a cathartic effect, but with Catullus this is not the case: suffering is not healed by poetry.[27] This new approach to poetry is disturbing and leads to the result that the strongly erotic discussions and poetic images verging on the obscene change into platitudes and also into verses that even Cicero was willing to have chiseled on his *pergula:*

> Soles occidere et redire possunt;
> Nobis cum semel occidit brevis lux
> Nox est perpetua una dormienda.[28]

The old world finds it disturbing that the beginning and the end of a poem do not present a clear and recognizable context of thought, and that a new, nascent symbolism has emerged, the meaning of which can be perhaps guessed but not firmly defined. Cicero writes to Pomponius (in a passage which is not based on any historical documents, and in which Wilder can be seen leveling a criticism at the lyric poetry of his own time) : "If we are to be condemned to a poetry based on buried trains of thought, my dear Pomponius, we shall soon be at the mercy of the unintelligible parading about among us as a superior mode of sensibility." [29]

For the conservative Cicero, the spirit is the marketplace where the slave and the philosopher rub shoulders, or, as he expresses it elsewhere, the rose and the weed grow side by side. In the spirit, the trivial every moment encounters the sublime.[30] For six hundred years after Homer it was the poets' task to penetrate chaos. Then this task was given up. It is not by chance that the conservative sees a connection between the decay of literature and the decay of the state. "The maintenance of categories is the health not only of literature, but of the State." [31] It cannot be by accident that the head of such a state does not see the problem of the decay of poetry in his time at all.

Herein lies Catullus' difficulty. He has a vision of freedom; he combats the dictator; he conspires with the conservatives in politics; in poetry he represents the liberation from and the dissolution of the old forms, and his poems are esteemed by the dictator himself. Catullus is the exponent of the "new poetry" and at the same time probably the only one among the Roman intellectuals who still takes passion seriously. Such a mosaic of tendencies and views offers various possibilities for a reactionary regrouping.

Poetry is not only a matter of technique and practice, although it is in part this, for Catullus as for other poets. To Clodia's jibe that he has not succeeded with a single poem, Catullus replies that almost always, even for the best of poets, only a few verses succeed by inspiration while the rest require the work of creation.[32]

Now the genesis of a poem is not especially relevant to the problem of the results of poetry. It does not especially affect the claim that poetry is divine, a claim that is discussed at a central point of the novel. Just after the first attempt on Caesar's life, the dictator, Catullus, and Clodia Pulcher meet to discuss the meaning of poetry. This scene is cast by Wilder in the form of a long letter from Asinius Pollio to Vergil and Horace. Asinius Pollio is portrayed as moderate in temperament and is meant as a guarantee of objectivity. Wilder further emphasizes this by having Pollio's report replace the one allegedly prepared by Caesar, which is omitted because of its subjectivity.

It is Pollio's task to recite the usual arguments of the ancients in behalf of poetry: that it comes from the gods, that—like love—it is a thing possessed and therefore more than human. Everything that is human—so runs the argument—is destroyed by time, but not poetry. Poetry, by its survival, legitimizes its claim to divinity.

To this argument Clodia is the destructive opponent. Her disillusioning argument is that poetry makes man childish, distorts his view of reality, and creates the illusory perspectives that he needs in order to face the world. It is significant, she continues, that the fable of the Golden Fleece was created by the poets. Poetry occupies the commanding heights above man's conceptual world and thus makes possible the disguising of political aims.

Clodia also points out that the poet, whatever else is passed down by tradition concerning him, is regarded as unrealistic; this—she declares—is sufficiently attested by the anecdotes about Sophocles and Menander. The discussion also treats the question of whether poetry is a means of penetrating into the metaphysical realm, and to this Clodia says that the poet has no such insight as was claimed for him: he leads astray by unrealistic imagery and beclouds those insights that man has already achieved.

The idea of poetry as a proof of God Clodia finds especially detestable. One can well believe that the gods no longer trouble themselves about the world, but it is too horrible to imagine that the gods, through the agency of poets, wish to deceive man as to his true condition. For Clodia Pulcher, haunted as she is by the memory of being raped as a young girl, the poet too must have had a trauma in his youth which has created in him a cosmic anxiety that he seeks to master by indulging in fantasy.

Catullus'—and Wilder's—reaction to this is significant. Instead of counter-arguments, he invokes the mythological figure of Alcestis. He does not do this arrogantly or pompously. He mentions how familiar the story is: "Every child knows. . . ." [33] He then calmly and thoroughly relates the story, giving it a few new highlights.

The old mythological matter is not automatically adopted on faith. When Admetus tells Alcestis that Apollo was present in his mind and was teaching him how to harness together a lion and a boar and thus win Alcestis as his bride, her rejoinder is positively rationalistic: ". . . There is no lack of reports about the Gods from the delirium of young men and the tales of old nurses. It is just such stories which have increased the confusion in which all men live." [34]

Alcestis wishes to overcome all that and be herself close to the god in Delphi. Then Jupiter's messenger appears and proclaims that Apollo in the form of a shepherd is outside the walls. It is not given to her to recognize Apollo; the temptation with a miracle does not lead to this knowledge. The singer among the five shepherds appears so questionable that he is hardly to be identified with Apollo. "He loses joy in the thing he has made and is in labor to fashion another. That is enough to assure me that he is not a God, nor even a messenger of the Gods, for the Gods cannot be thought of as despising their handiwork." [35] It would be naïve to judge the manifestation of the divine on the basis of signs that are the idealizing work of the human spirit.

Poetry leads to analyses of the divine. But the act of thinking and experiencing cannot produce a knowledge of the
divine, but rather an increasing mysteriousness that is bound
up with religious feeling.

One of the novel's tensest scenes closes this chapter.
As Catullus resumes his discourse with the words, "You may
well imagine . . . ," Caesar has an attack of epilepsy.[36]
The closing words of the discourse remain unsaid, perhaps
necessarily so. The majesty of the divine sickness puts everyone in awe. The effect of the sickness on Caesar is ambigu-
ous. For reasons of state it does not suit him that there
should be much public discussion of the malady. Even
among his closer entourage no one, with few exceptions, is
permitted to speak of it. But the illness has also a happy
impulse for him, for he experiences inner harmony, a counterpoise to the dream of emptiness.

> This nothingness, however, does not present itself to us as a
> blank and a quiet, but as a total evil unmasked. It is at once
> laughter and menace. It turns into ridicule all delights and sears
> and shrivels all endeavor. This dream is the counterpart of that
> vision which comes to me in the paroxysm of my illness. Then I
> seem to grasp the fair harmony of the world. I am filled with
> unspeakable happiness and confidence. I wish to cry out to all
> the living and all the dead that there is no part of the universe
> that is untouched by bliss.[37]

The contradictory and two-sided experience of emptiness
and harmony finds a sort of correlative in the experience of
good and evil. Elsewhere in the total context of the novel, it
is also connected to the love between Clodia and Catullus.

"At the closer range we say good and evil, but what the
world profits by is intensity. There is a law hidden in this,
but we are not present long enough to glimpse more than
two links in the chain. There lies the regret at the brevity of

life."[38] At a later point Caesar no longer places the main
accent on intensity, nor does he any longer express regret
and resignation that man is not permitted to see farther
than two links in the chain of life. Caesar's scope of knowledge, meanwhile, has not grown broader. The incomprehensible more and more afflicts the scope of his vision. The
sphere of life removed from reason gives him certainty:

> —Yet of both of them the mind says: henceforth this I know.
> They cannot be dismissed as illusions. To each our memory
> brings many a radiant and many a woeful corroboration. We
> cannot disown the one without disowning the other, nor would
> I—like a village peacemaker reconciling the differences of two
> contending parties—accord to each a shrunken measure of the
> right.[39]

It is always those areas of life in which man is unsure of
himself that lead Caesar into the realm of metaphysics. The
process often begins with something rational, such as his
reforms of the College of Augurs, and ends—in his case, for
he is not a thinker—in knowledge through shock. One of
those areas in which man is no longer sure of himself is love,
which Caesar explains as the most immediate phenomenon
of shock. Caesar thinks about religious processes partly in
connection with erotic ones. In his imagination he sees
himself as a young priest of Jove at the side of Cornelia.

The great encounters with women in the novel have
overtones of the mystery of the world. Such are the meeting
with Cleopatra in Rome, Catullus' love for Clodia Pulcher,
Caesar's marriage to Pompeia and later to Calpurnia.
Wilder has further accentuated the meaning of the erotic by
having negative outcomes parallel each other. Caesar's love
for Cleopatra is destroyed in the moment of its fulfillment.
At the same time Catullus dies, his love for Clodia shattered. Clodia has become Lesbia for him, and his life in its

intensity raises the question of the forces that begin to take shape in love.

Catullus' love has the effect of paradox: the love he has known gains its great fame through his poetry, but the love experience is dissolved in incitement and denial. The image he constructs cannot be realized. Before it is destroyed from within, his love for Clodia is for him the humanly divine activation of *eros:* When I looked at you the God Eros descended upon me. I was more than myself. The God lived in me, looked through my eyes and spoke through my lips." [40] Later, too, Catullus is constrained to go on believing in the power of Eros, although he also comes to believe that power is already on its way to dissolution the very moment it appears.

The duality of the promise of fulfillment on the one hand and of the renunciation of knowledge on the other appears also in the hour of Catullus' death. He regrets that he has been unable to attain to knowledge, and at the same time gives expression to praise of the road he has taken in the dark. Here again Catullus points to the fate of Sophocles, to whom the gods neither offered nor refused help although they gave him no help in actuality. Their remaining hidden spurred his impulse to attain to knowledge: "If they were not hidden he would not so have peered to find them." [41]

The result is, inevitably, another paradox: The one sure result of knowledge striving for the preservation of the world is that we must renounce the idea of any clear knowledge and therefore of that security which ultimate knowledge seems to offer as promise and consolation. The paradox was strongly evident in the structure of the Second Book. Offense taken at superstition and its forms had led to the question of what was concealed in superstition and thereby to the religious problem generally. Caesar wanted to be the supreme pontiff not only in name but also in fact. This led him into skepticism and on through awe to a new beginning of faith. Caesar, as an active man, receives as the last fruit of his earthly existence the possibility of reflection, and this brings with it skepticism as to the correctness of his own decisions. This reflection, however, has a very short span of life. The opening document of *The Ides of March* is a message to the Master of the College of Augurs, concerning a restriction of their functions. It is dated September 1, 45. The same date appears on Document 60 in the Fourth Book, a chain letter calling for Caesar's assassination. Caesar's approaching death overshadows the entire action, which extends over not more than a half year.

The purification process in the case of a religious person—psychologically analogous to the effect of awe— seeks to restrict the substance of the divine to the concept "mind." ". . . The principal attribute of the Gods is mind . . ." [42] which is covered over by the forms of superstition which confront Caesar both in Rome and elsewhere. Caesar, being unpractical in thinking, is not able to declare what the nature of "mind" is. He supports its freedom despite his dictatorial power of authority: "Imprisonment of the body is bitter; imprisonment of the mind is worse." [43] Catullus, whose creation of the beautiful challenges the world, suffers a "long crucifixion of the mind." [44] The gods, to whom the liberation of the spirit is supposed to lead man, are able also to restrict the adventure of the spirit, and the actress Cytheris speaks of the blessing of this restriction in a letter to Lucius Mamilius Turrinus.

In the structure of the novel, besides these reflections on the nature of religion and the divine, there are plot features of a great cathartic quality. There is the attempt on Caesar's life, which leads to Catullus' tale of Alcestis and thus to the essential recognition that a man-made norm can never help illuminate the nature of the divine. The Cleopatra episode, the profanation of the Mysteries of the Good Goddess, and finally the assassination on the Ides of March are further emphases of this kind in the plot structure.

The renewed road to divinity and religion is the road of revealing and veiling, as in great poetry or in love. Love became effective in the negative state above all, when the love that man has known is destroyed from within, and when man is moved at the thought of transitoriness and the experiences of denial. Here the need to remain in faith becomes a manifestation of the power of the divine.

In the design of the novel all this shows the great significance of man in a state of suffering and being driven by his emotion. Thus Wilder in *The Ides of March* again employs one of his favorite constructions: A person who is not first and foremost a thinker—such as the padre in *The Bridge of San Luis Rey*—is drawn by a decisive situation into thinking, and in doing so perceives where thinking has its limits: on the boundary of religious knowledge.

In *The Ides of March*, the genus of the historical novel is used as both foil and pretext. The documentary and pseudo-documentary forms provide the objective "framework." To provide objectivity the author contrasts Cicero and Cornelius Nepos with the acting and suffering Caesar. Cicero conceives of the world from the intellectual-historical standpoint, but he is influenced by the urge to self-importance and by psychological reactions. Cornelius Nepos, on the other hand, is the chronicler who simply records—at least, Wilder represents him as such, without giving weight to the fact that the Roman historians of the Empire saw in him the critical observer of his own time. In this way Wilder can have Suetonius cite Cornelius Nepos as authority for all items of gossip concerning the questionable and petty side of human nature.

The two historians' modes of viewing, presenting and reacting to the events they narrate are contrasted by Wilder's use of two consecutive documents: Document 33, "Cornelius Nepos' Commonplace Book," containing the two entries of October 3 and 4, and Document 33 A, "Cicero in Rome to his Brother." The report of Cornelius Nepos begins with the objective statement that "the Queen has arrived." It continues in short sentences, reporting second-hand information with such phrases as "is reported to be" and "gossip report," and giving eyewitness impressions with a clear definition of the witness' standpoint: ". . . To me at a distance she seemed . . ." and ". . . Alina having a better view of advantage and being a woman reports . . ."

Cicero begins at once with subjective reactions: "The words 'Queen of Egypt' cast a deep spell, my friend, but not upon me." He is unwilling to be the dupe: "Her walk and port is much admired but not by me." Instead of observing, he seeks at once to classify her according to his theory ("I indulge a theory that . . .") and finally he again admonishes: "One must be on the alert to recognize these things, however. The prestige of her title; the magnificence of her dress; the effect of her two signal advantages—namely, her fine eyes and the beauty of her speaking voice—subdue."

The interesting thing about Cicero is not his comic mannerisms, his personal cowardice, nor his anxious conservatism. It is rather that this sentimental person is unable to exceed the bounds fixed in him by sentiment, but instead labors permanently under the reaction of resentment. He regards Catullus' split in the ego as a barbaric threat, but he sees for himself no possibility of gaining access to the other ego.

Document 26 A, showing Catullus tortured by subjective grief, is answered with a passage from the Commonplace Book of Cornelius Nepos, giving Cicero's view of Catullus' new kind of poetry. Honest Cornelius Nepos obviously does not know what to make of Catullus' poetry, and finds it strange that Catullus has such subjective poems circulate from hand to hand. He notes with some amazement: "I can think of no precedent for so candid a revelation." Cicero is extremely agitated over the dialogue quality of this poetry: "Whose is this other voice that is so often addressing him— this voice that urges him to 'bear up' and to 'pull himself together'? Is that his genius? Is that some other-self?" [45]

Cicero can find no access to this poetry, because to do so would mean having to give up his specific ego-bias. He therefore prefers to concern himself more with the political and cultural consequences of such a poetry as that of Catullus than with the poetry itself.—It is also revealing that his position as letter-writer, in this novel consisting mainly of letters, is largely dehumanized. Document 31, a letter to Atticua in Greece, is meant to give a hint of humanity. Misfortune in love and marriage, which makes Cicero into a perfect and respected malcontent, draw general observations from him without making him appear as a real human being. If Cornelius Nepos' hallmark is naïve objectivity, the hallmark of Cicero is the pseudo-objectivity that, by shielding him from all genuine human engagement, allows him to live for his own ego.

For the egocentric as well as for the naïve, the lyric of Catullus is incomprehensible. Cornelius Nepos' friendship is vouched for, and yet wretched is a mild word for what the historian has to say about the poet.—Caesar senses far more of the meaning of Catullus' lyrics, and so does the actress Cytheris. Their respective positions in life, their successes and triumphs, could not have made such an understanding exactly easy for them. Catullus' lyric poetry discloses to them an awareness of the limits of the ego. To the trials of character that this involves they show themselves equal, both in character and in intellect. The really great human beings in this book prove to be frank in their relations with others: in respect and liking, in friendship, in love. They know therefore what it is to feel obligated and thus inevitably get into a condition of great vulnerability. In the case of the most intelligent, such as the actress Cytheris, this condition is mastered the most effectively. In a letter to Lucius Mamilius Turrinus, Cytheris says plainly that the greatest years of her life were those of her intimate love for Marc Antony and that her friendship for Turrinus is a great good, but, for her as a woman, not the highest.

Catullus is now haunted and buffeted about by erotic encounters. The woman of his longings, Clodia Pulcher, is a prostitute of whom the writings on the walls of Rome tell the worst there is to tell. What Wilder reports concerning this is mostly in accord with the historical facts (cf. Documents 2, 2 A, and 5). Her prostitution is confirmed numerous times in the ancient writers, as is also her extreme propensity for intrigue. In his poetry Catullus projects Clodia Pulcher into another reality: she is his Lesbia, a name meant to be reminiscent of Sappho. In life Clodia Pulcher embodies the distortion of all good human ideas; in poetry she is the embodiment of Catullus' illusion: "Catullus . . . apparently regards his relations with Clodia Pulcher— relations which he never mentions in conversation—as a pure and lofty love which no one could confuse with the ephemeral loves in which his friends are continuously involved," [46] writes Cornelius Nepos in his Commonplace Book.

Asinius Pollio notes in a letter: "That Valerius should love this woman with such intensity and for so long a time has caused consternation in all who know him. . . . When he talks of her he seems to be talking of someone we have never known . . . Valerius tells my brother of her wisdom, her kindness to the unfortunate, the delicacy of her sympathy, her greatness of soul. I have known her for many years; I enjoy her company; but I am never unaware that she hates the air she breathes and everything and everyone about her." [47]

The release and redemption of Clodia from her perversions Catullus consummates in himself. It would be a mistake to regard this process as an abstraction, as Asinius Pollio does. Clodia too regards it in this way when she writes to Catullus: "You have not been writing to me but to that image of me lodged in your head whom I have no wish to confront." [48]

The secret of Catullus' greatness and failure in his love for Clodia Pulcher lies in its unconditional and unreserved quality, which places him in the position of a vassal. In this situation he tells her: "No one has ever talked about the stars as you talk about them. I worship you always, but then you are all Goddess . . . Great queen, greater than all the queens of Egypt, wise and good, learned and gracious. . . ." [49]

It is not that Catullus fails to see the scandalous side of Clodia's life. Wilder represents him as irreproachable in his mode of living. Cornelius Nepos notes the same,[50] and Asinius Pollio notes it still more plainly: "Catullus . . . is astonishingly strict in his life and in his judgments of the lives of others." [51] When it is a question of criticizing morals in degenerate Rome, Catullus is deterred neither by rank nor by position. His hatred of Caesar, whose love affairs and homosexual tendencies he discusses, is by no means essentially political. And in his letters Catullus occasionally makes strong accusations against Clodia. Nothing of this is known to the outside world, excepting Caesar, whose surveillance system makes such documents available to him. The worshipper and the vassal see only that which is worthy of love and reverent preservation. This of course has little in common with the historical Catullus. Wilder makes Catullus the spokesman for a view that sees in love one of the means that lead human knowledge to the realm of metaphysics. If one wished to seek in Greek literature for an exponent of such a view, one would have to cite the relevant passage in Plato's *Symposium*.

The tragic fact that his idealistically conceived passion is incapable of fulfillment is what shatters Catullus. His personal life is destroyed by the basic antinomy between the wish for separateness and the wish for unity, and its antinomic consequences that find their expression in ruling and being ruled, torturing and suffering, destroying and preserving, falling sick, and seeking that which is whole. In the dichotomy between seeing love as the ideal process of attaining to knowledge and, on the other hand, being tortured by the pains of love, Catullus writes the verses that place him beyond this cleavage:

> Ille mi par esse deo videtur,
> Ille, si fas est, superare divos . . .[52]

Caesar also grasps in an emergency the support offered by these lines of Catullus. He too is haunted by passion, but it does not destroy him completely as it does Catullus. The didactic and—sometimes ironically—schoolmasterish element in him is emphasized repeatedly in various documents of the novel. Cytheris—who, in contrast to her bad name in Roman history, is portrayed by Wilder as an intellectually superior and perceptive person (possibly for the sake of dramatic effect in the scenes in which she appears) —alludes to love's wonderful educational effect. Only in performing this function can love create harmony, but its equilibrium is then so unstable that a disturbance of it can create complete chaos.

Caesar seeks to avoid the tragedy and, by a kind of

sublimation in serious play-acting, to preserve the continuance that can save the situation. But the acting slips into
real tragedy, as Cytheris reports to Lucius Mamilius Turrinus: "We have had eight sessions, frequently concluded by
readings from the tragedies in which we all take part,
including Caesar himself. I find myself moving in a tragedy
within a tragedy." [53]

Caesar, who is by nature committed to the rule of order
in extensive areas of life, knows of the intensity which alone
can give to experience its value as knowledge. At maximum
intensity, however, such an experience must develop into a
mortal sickness. Love can never be a human possession,
much less a human property. Catullus, and Caesar once,
have experienced it in a "high noon," and Cytheris has
known it for fifteen decisive years of her life. In this period
the relationship to the secret of the world is achieved; man
has become conscious of awe, of knowledge in the Goethean
sense, without being able to unlock the secret of awe himself.

In passages like this, Wilder's characterizations in this
work are in the strongest and perhaps the happiest combination with his ideology. In this way the ideology—which
is conscious and, as we have seen, unhistorical—is human-
ized into a thing of flesh and blood. This entire novel of
Wilder's with its elements of history and life is marked by
the duality of the abstract and the living. Side by side with
fundamental reflections are penetrating pictures of the everyday life of antiquity. This is made clearer by a statement of
Wilder's concerning the nature and aims of creative writing:
"Story-telling ability springs not . . . from an aversion to
general ideas but from an instinctive coupling of idea and
illustration: the idea for a born storyteller can only be
embedded in its circumstantial illustrations. Modern taste
shrinks from emphasizing the central idea that hides behind
the fiction." [54]

Wilder does not shrink from making a very plain statement of the "theses," and in doing so often harks back to the classical heritage. The characterizations, with their strong cases of isolation and of failure, are not unaffected by modern Existentialism, and the same is in some measure true of the occasional triviality. Caesar comments in Document 59 B: "Yet our lives are immersed in the trivial; the significant comes to us enwrapped in multitudinous details of the trivial; the trivial has this dignity, that it exists and is omnipresent." [55]

Not all of *The Ides of March* has to do with these trivia: dog breeding, canal installations, a secret hair-growing formula and dozens of other such things. They convey the local color and the human everyday life of antiquity. But they show at the same time the junction and the polarity of human existence, of which we have become again so intensely aware in recent decades. Antiquity has here become the background for a feeling that is very much a part of modern life.

≺ 6 ≻

Our Town

WILDER'S first major play appeared in 1938. He had occupied himself with the drama before that, but the results at most were tentative: one-act pieces that ran to just a few pages in length, and adaptations of foreign plays such as André Obey's *Le Viol de Lucrèce*.

Wilder's earlier attempts at drama had prompted in him reflections on literary theory. The plays of Obey offered many stimuli. The theatrical group to which Obey belonged, the Compagnie de Quinze, staged experimental plays in the years 1930 to 1936, and some of its members were also associated with the Théâtre du Vieux Colombier, which Wilder often visited. Obey was what Wilder very much aspired to be, an actor-manager. He had experimented with a variety of dramatic styles, and had employed themes not remote from Wilder's own. His *Lucrèce* was written in the style of Greek tragedy, with copious use of chorus and commentators, and his play *Noé* treated the theme of the Deluge.

The impulses that Wilder received through the French theater were enlarged by his foreign travel. This meant a great deal in the nineteen-twenties and nineteen-thirties, for the European theater was then experiencing a great enthusiasm for experiment: the expressionist drama and the political play in Berlin, Pirandello's concept of the theater brought to the public, the people's play in Vienna.

A brief reference to these theatrical *Wanderjahre* of Wilder seems necessary if we are to avoid a distorted view of *Our Town* and *The Skin of Our Teeth,* which must be seen against the history of the contemporary theater. Both plays when they first appeared were judged by European critics primarily as experimental pieces, and some American critics too believed that *Our Town* owed its success to its "stunt quality." [1]

In Europe many regarded *Our Town* as the prelude—in its form, or its disintegration of form, depending on one's point of view—to *The Skin of Our Teeth.* In the sequence of performances of Wilder's plays in Germany, *The Skin of Our Teeth* often preceded *Our Town,* and the audience viewed the latter play as a mild prelude to, or a mere part of the prehistory of, *The Skin of Our Teeth.*

Apart from its—admittedly important—formal aspect, *Our Town* does not represent anything positively new in American literature. Since Edgar Lee Masters treated it in lyric form in his *Spoon River Anthology* (1915), the small town has become one of modern America's favorite literary themes. It achieved an almost worldwide fame with Sinclair Lewis' *Babbitt* and *Main Street,* and it continued after Lewis to provide a ready illustration of boredom, banality, endless repetition—the very themes that largely determined the existentialist literature in America. In the small town, though there too man is concerned with the business of living, he is not so absorbed in the struggle for existence as he is in the large American city. The latter received its decisive treatment with Dreiser, after significant beginnings by Herrick, Crane, Poole and Howells.[2]

The small community that Wilder portrays in *Our*

Town is of course one that is almost in a preserved state. The stage manager's comments place us in the year 1938, or the present, i.e., the time of the particular performance. But the actual life of this small town transpires between the years 1901 and 1913, so that the town is spared the effects of the most recent industrial trends. Today's small town—unlike the Grover's Corners of the play—has each its own daily police report and its own incidence of vice, and not just in the form of a drunkard like Simon Stimson. Simon is himself middle class, and the town society ignores or glosses over his frailty; many details about him we learn only after his death.

Though it was written at a time when sociology plays a great role in America as elsewhere, and though its title would lead one to expect matter of sociological interest, the play's strictly sociological side is not too important. In part that aspect is even treated ironically by the stage manager, in part it is handled by questioning and by interjected calls from members of the cast who are placed out in the audience. The figure of the rustic Professor Willard, with his pedantry and scientific circumlocution, underscores the ironic manner. Willard's statements on geology and demography lend of course a certain natural-science and social-science aspect to the content, but this is unquestionably not the dramatist's essential aim.

Now and again one can gather further sociological data from the action of the play, as for example the fact that this small New England town has a proletarian or semi-proletarian Polish quarter with its own present or potential social problems. All this is, however, much less important than the world of the little man. That world definitely extends into the academic class, and indeed has in that class its model exemplification. In its external life it is strongly absorbed in its professional concerns. Yet it is not so lost in meditation but that its actions and especially its words bring home to the audience the little man's concern with the great questions of youth, marriage, and death, so that the observer—if he is not socially biased—can identify himself with these people. The play gains life thereby, though it is a life that seems much reduced by the absence of many of the external features to which the average playgoer is still very much accustomed.

His first surprise awaits him in the appearance of the stage itself, uncurtained and open. In this play bourgeois drama's box-sets are dispensed with. Furnishings are either eliminated or replaced by a few token articles of furniture that merely suggest to the audience's imagination that which is missing.

With such sets as these, Wilder showed his decided opposition to the traditional box-set stage. In this he was by no means alone; in Europe a movement against the box-set stage had begun with the advent of expressionistic drama about 1910. This current became noticeable in the American theater in the nineteen-twenties, first in the great dramas of O'Neill and then in the plays of Elmer Rice and some lesser-known authors. For a time, however, its influence remained rather limited.

Wilder repeatedly took issue with the traditional three-walled stage, particularly in an article that Longmans, Green & Co. subsequently published in the volume *Three Plays*. In this article Wilder tells how in the nineteen-twenties he lost his love of the theater, how he found the stage offerings unbelievable and regretted that the theater did not make use of its natural possibilities.[3]

These possibilities derived naturally from the purposes of drama, which must avoid outward features which distract and confuse, if the audience is to recognize in the play its own situation. As Wilder observes, it is no coincidence that in the nineteenth century the middle class avoided just this. It was because it hated the passions that it gave such a strong affirmation to the theater of illusion in the form of the box-set stage. For Wilder, on the other hand, the aim is to employ the illusion-destroying media of the drama and stage. Only by these means can the *degagé* audience, produced by the old-style theater, be eliminated.

Drama offers Wilder the opportunity to bring his literary anthropology to the fore. In his reflections on the principles of drama he also stresses this by reverting to the differences between the novel and the drama: the novel individualizes, the drama typifies. To be sure, the individual too has its significance in drama, but in addition there is the repetitive pattern which orients the audience to generalities.

The bare stage, which is ready for these essential things, is, therefore, one of Wilder's basic demands. In a modification of Molière's saying that a couple of boards and one or two passions were all he needed for a drama, Wilder asks for five square feet of planks and the "passion to know what life means to us." [4] In *Our Town* the props have been reduced to a minimum. A few chairs and tables serve as the kitchen, stepladders suggest different floors, and a plank serves as the bar. A few rows of chairs stand for graves. More rows of chairs, together with the projection of a small lancet window on the stage's back wall, represent the village church.

In all this the audience is not left in the dark as to the fact that many of these hints are merely aids for those persons who are lacking in imagination. The stage manager announces ironically that there is also a furnished stage for those who need that sort of thing. And the stage is completely without props when Emily returns to earth to re-live her twelfth birthday.

Accentuating the bareness of the stage is the fact that the

usual activity of the actors has been replaced by pantomime. The drama of our time has helped revive this art; Brecht and Claudel have employed it in some of their plays. The French had the added advantage that in recent decades they had among their actors some outstanding artists of pantomime. Wilder became familiar with the significance of pantomime for the drama especially through the Oriental theater, in particular the Japanese Nô-plays, which found an interested audience in America.

What at first glance seems in *Our Town* to be a rather arbitrary experiment or whimsical primitiveness, are expressions of Wilder's dramatic concept, which takes issue with the technique of drama and stagecraft that has evolved in the theater.

Another illusion-destroying feature—as seen by the tradition-minded theatergoer—is the prominence accorded to the stage manager, with his many and varied functions in introducing, accompanying and concluding the play.

The drama begins with these words, spoken by the stage manager:

> This play is called *Our Town*. It was written by Thornton Wilder; produced and directed by A. . . . (or: produced by A. . . . ; directed by B. . . .). In it you will see Miss C. . . . ; Miss D. . . . ; Miss E. . . . ; and Mr. F. . . . ; Mr. G. . . . ; Mr. H. . . . ; and many others. The name of the town is Grover's Corners, New Hampshire,—just across the Massachusetts line: longitude 42 degrees 40 minutes; latitude 70 degrees 37 minutes. The First Act shows a day in our town. The day is May 7, 1901. The time is just before dawn.[5]

These lines perform the function that the program does in the usual kind of play. They name the author, director, and actors, and the place and time of the action. But here again is an admixture of irony: the exact geographical location of

Grover's Corners ("longitude 42 degrees 40 minutes; latitude 70 degrees 37 minutes" [6]) is given with a scientific
pedantry that also emerges at other points of the play and is
a gentle satire on a certain primitive kind of realism.

But in these comic didactic pedantries (including those
of Professor Willard on geology) there is at the same time a
kernel of significance for the play's broad design. It is that
everything with which the play is concerned, though small
in itself, is embedded in a great context; it is as old as stone,
and is firmly placed in the order of the world and the
universe.

Leaning casually against the proscenium pillar and
smoking his pipe, the stage manager lets the professional
people speak and supply the exposition. What was the
function of dialogue in classical drama is here left entirely
to the stage manager. In addition he has the task of an-
nouncing the individual acts and giving each its title. At the
beginning of the Second Act he divides up the play as
follows: "The First Act was called the Daily Life. This Act
is called Love and Marriage. There's another Act coming
after this: I reckon you can guess what that's about." [7]

By addressing the public directly, the stage manager
destroys the usual separation between the stage and the
audience. Just as in many novels the author, from his
vantage point of knowledge, converses with his reader, so
also the omniscient and omnipotent stage manager talks
very familiarly with his audience. This familiarity is seen in
his encouraging phrases and rhetorical questions, and in the
way he occasionally addresses the audience as "folks" or
"friends," a form of address that Wilder is rather fond of
using in his own lectures. Occasionally the stage manager
turns to a specific group in the audience; thus when a
kitchen scene is played on the stage, he addresses the housewives. Nor is he the only character in this play who speaks

directly to the public; the newspaper publisher Webb does too in his general discussion concerning the town.

Wilder would probably like best a full and spontaneous participation by the audience in various scenes of the play. This would mean an end to audience passivity and the liquidation of the old-style theater. Such attempts were also made by other authors at the end of the nineteen-twenties and the beginning of the thirties, but they foundered on the fact that today's audience is unsuited to such experiments.

In *Our Town,* to overcome the gap between the stage and the audience, players are concealed among the audience. Examples are the lady in the balcony who asks about alcoholism in Grover's Corners, the lady in the loge who inquires as to the state of culture there, and the class-conscious and argumentative man in the second balcony who poses deep politico-social questions.

In the staging of *Our Town*—and not only here—we see Wilder's efforts to eliminate the old barriers. Steps and gangways lead down into the audience, and these are used. The Elizabethan stage, especially the apron stage, may have given Wilder a number of ideas.

The stage manager has also to introduce the characters. In this role he is a kind of announcer, a figure that is not without its precedent in the theater, going back to the medieval plays. But in addition to his being an announcer, his words reveal a knowledge of the future fates of the characters in the play.

The stage manager has great power to arrange his world, but at the same time he is himself in this world. He speaks of "our town," and his words are the usual American colloquial speech, with its easy careless informality. They put him on the same plane as the audience. Where it seems to him necessary, the stage manager takes the part of one of the characters. In the ballgame scene he is the admonishing

Mrs. Hicks, at the double wedding he is the clergyman, and in the early love scenes between George and Emily he is the drugstore soda clerk.

The stage manager not only assumes these roles in the play; he also occasionally reflects upon them. Thus when he plays the clergyman, he remarks that in this role he would be better able to comment on the play. He then mentions the confusion of feelings which is usual at weddings and must be included in such a play.

> In this wedding I play the minister. That gives me the right to say a few more things about it. For a while now the play gets pretty serious. Y'see, some churches say that marriage is a sacrament. I don't quite know what that means, but I can guess. Like Mrs. Gibbs said a few minutes ago: People were made to live two-by-two. This is a good wedding, but people are so put together that even at a good wedding there's a lot of confusion way down deep in people's minds and we thought that that ought to be in our play, too.[8]

The epic quality, to which the stage manager is already predisposed, and which is further accentuated in his character by the everyday plot, is made distinct in the very play itself by the stage manager's words we have just quoted. The play's surface—solid in the traditional theater—has taken on a transparent quality.

The special character of the play conducted by the stage manager is also brought out by his thanking the players after each scene.[9] He signals to players from behind the scenes when he thinks they are exceeding the bounds of good taste, as when George's baseball teammates make suggestive remarks before the wedding.

More important is the question of what effect Wilder expects the structural change made in a play by the stage manager to have on the development of the drama of his time. Undoubtedly the stage manager relieves the dialogue of some of its burden, at least the burden of all those external things that the realistic problem drama had introduced in the nineteenth century. To the British and American reader, schooled by George Bernard Shaw, this innovation would naturally appeal. Freed from this ballast, the dialogue—especially in *Our Town*, can address itself especially to human relations. But Wilder does not treat these relations at all in the way that the old romantic and poetic drama did. In Wilder these human relations signify rather a kind of Christian anthropology.

Wilder, who began as a teacher, makes no secret of the fact that he would like to be a kind of *praeceptor mundi*— not with arrogance but humility, yet with all the decisiveness that now stands behind his conception of the world. The stage manager is also the didactic: ironic yet kind, forgiving and at the same time educating.

In another connection Wilder, telling of the origin of the stage manager within the framework of his own writings, called him a "hangover from a novelist technique." [10] This clearly is to say that the stage manager is an epic factor within Wilder's drama. Peter Szondi believes that the preliminary stage to this epic ego, in the development of the drama, was Strindberg's *Ghosts,* in which one of the characters from the start has knowledge of all the others. This figure corresponds to the epic, omniscient narrator in the novel.[11] To mere drama—not to say bare drama—there is added a figure who enlarges and explains the view of things, and, at times, also verbally embellishes it. This figure, though it naturally tends to be illusion-destroying, also appeals to man's illusion when it is a question of clarifying his existence. The stage manager can even recall the dead to the land of the living—something that in *The Woman of Andros* only Zeus could do.

Apart from these things, the stage manager in *Our Town*

introduces ordinary middle-class Americans who believe that
they are leading an individual life, and who would like to
create the same illusion in those around them. Of course,
he does not bring this life with all its varied activities im
mediately into the metaphysical sphere—which in Wilder's
opinion is not so easy to achieve—but rather brings them
into relation with general values. It is therefore characteristic that he does not ask, "How did the love beween George
and Emily begin?" but rather "How do such things begin?" [12] This question concerns a basic human condition and
not an actual social situation.

The meaning of such a question, which appears simple
enough, is illuminated by another element in the design of
this play. If it smacked of paradox that a play designed to
reduce drama to its most elementary parts had an epic element introduced into it, it is even more of a paradox that
in a play which is apparently the product of hyper-modern
experimentalism, the three classical unities are observed,
even if not very strictly. The action of *Our Town* takes place
entirely in Grover's Corners. There are no real subsidiary
plots—the bare stage, to begin with, restricts any such possibilities, and the time is so skillfully distributed over the
three acts that one gains the impression that the classical
"unity of time" is still in effect. It is true that the three acts
take place on three different days, but the entire play is so
designed for effect that it begins with a cock-crow, and ends
with the stage manager bidding the audience goodnight in
something like the role of a night watchman.

The individual acts of the play and the simple human
activities in them give us the schedule of life in this town. At
5:45 A.M. is the departing whistle of the early train to
Boston; soon after that the deliveries of milk and news-
papers; then the mothers get up to make the children's
breakfast; and the children go to school.

All this is presented to us in an exceedingly familiar way

by means of whistles, ringing of bells, and calling. Yet the end effect has a certain subtlety: the audience has the impression of the constant passage of a segment of time. But this span of time moves in small time units. The view of time expressed in this First Act of *Our Town* is elucidated by a passage in one of Wilder's early works. In *Pullman Car Hiawatha* the stage manager says that the minutes are gossips, the hours philosophers, and the years theologians. This is paralleled in a later phase of Wilder's works, in *The Skin of Our Teeth,* where each of the late hours is interpreted by means of a passage from Spinoza, Plato, or Aristotle.

The First Act presents the time of bustling activity. The stage manager looks on all this with his watch in his hand. But the instrument that is man's best aid in reckoning time gives him no idea of the reality of time itself.

In the First Act the passage of time plays the great role. In Act Two there is, at the beginning, a reference to this in the fact that the attrition of time is made good by new births. Nature is the great adversary of time: "Nature's been pushing and contriving in other ways, too: a number of young people fell in love and got married." [13] There was a certain hint of this kind also in Act One that Wilder may even have meant mischievously, when we are told on Dr. Gibbs' first appearance that he is returning from the delivery of twins. This notation, incidentally, shows the stage manager is having a positively confusing knowledge of time in all its phases. Dr. Gibbs is introduced in one act that takes place in the year 1901. At the same time, however, the stage manager reports in the past tense that Dr. Gibbs died in 1930 and that later a hospital in town was named after him. The stage manager, the sapient one, has the present, past and future time equally at his disposal.

The Second Act has, however, another function. In Act One the Gibbs and Webb families live self-contained lives side by side with each other. Now they are linked together by the wedding of their children. A lasting bond has been created, which will, however, as we soon learn, be broken by the death of one of the parties. Time is not only a stream constantly flowing in small units; it also creates things that are final.

The key image in the plot of Act Two was the long middle aisle leading to the altar. In place of the parallel action of two families there is common action. In the Third Act there is again separation. The rows of chairs indicating graves dominate one side of the stage.

Wilder further emphasizes this theme of community and separation—sometimes ironically—by having the hymn "Blessed Be the Tie That Binds" played or sung four times. First it is sung in Act One by housewives at a church rehearsal. Then it is whistled by Emily's father when she tells him of the letter with the strange address. At the wedding of George and Emily (both of whom are very nervous before the ceremony) it is the choral hymn. Lastly, it is the hymn chosen for Emily's burial.

Finally, Wilder uses the play to illustrate his view of identity and time. It is precisely the interweaving of the everyday and the metaphysical world that serves to illuminate this question.

The entire play begins—as we saw—with a day that is not exceptional, indeed, a day of exemplary mediocrity; and the life of the characters has in its entire course nothing out of the ordinary, despite a few accents that are "of the hour." We know soon after the play has begun how everything is going to end, not because the play treats a familiar literary fable, but because it is a treatment of our ordinary life. There are hardly any differences in this usual sameness in the course of world history: in remote antiquity it is the same as in New England, we are told.[14] In its concrete details, and in its political behavior, daily life in the various periods of world history may have been different, but in its essential everyday manifestations it remains the same.

There were also so-called exciting factors for the generation living in the United States in the nineteen-thirties. The stage manager makes reference to the Versailles Treaty and to Lindbergh's flight across the ocean. But they are less important for evaluating the man of the time than is his everyday life, which determines him as an anthropological type. A play like *Our Town* which says something about this should be placed in the cornerstone of the new building when a new Bank of Grover's Corners is built, so that "people in those years from now will know a few simple facts about us."

Among these "simple facts" are the banal statements that are here set forth, and the conversations which are so simple in their words and content but are also, through an unerring instinct, so effective on the stage. An example of this is the almost identical conversations on the weather of May 9, 1901, July 7, 1901, and February 11, 1899. Truisms such as "It is unnatural to be alone" are repeated over and over in a number of variations, for in the final analysis the truisms rule the day.

The usual trend of American drama in Wilder's time seems in this play to have completely altered its direction. The abnormal, which so often dominated the stage, is here replaced by an almost unrelieved normality.

The play is largely without effect if the audience is not willing to identify itself with the play's content. To one who does make this identification, the "little world" of American academic life is his world, in which the so-called "events" have only an illustrative force. It is strange enough that the members of such a world should still place a value on identity. But the consciousness of identity is at the same time the force that keeps them attached to the old, and makes them so often timid toward every change. Reality is for them a life-devouring power of custom.

Personal identity in this play is not very strongly individualized; the author's characters largely run to type. At the very start, through the agency of the stage manager, Wilder reduces any excessive expectations. From these first statements, the audience cannot expect to find any extraordinary people in this play: "Nice town, y'know what I mean? Nobody very remarkable ever come out of it—s'far as we know." [15] The complete mediocrity of this town is clear from the somewhat euphemistic term "nice town," followed by the stage manager's rhetorical question as to an understanding between himself and the audience.

There are of course individual traits in George and Emily, but—as with Rebecca and Wally—they are made to typify youth; this is brought home to us all the more by the parallel scenes, in which almost the same words are used. The adults, too, have one common denominator: Mrs. Webb and Mrs. Gibbs in their almost complete absorption in their household cares, and Dr. Gibbs and Mr. Webb, who in their historical hobbies (the Napoleonic period, early American history) hardly differ from each other in any essential respect.[16]

But despite their extensive absorption in the type, the persons in the play continue to hold fast to their identity, which they lose only with death. Thereafter, to the outward eye, they continue to appear as bearers of one or another of the many Anglo-Saxon names—Gibbs, Webb, Hersey, etc. —until finally relegated to the alphabetical order of a cemetery. Inwardly, however, they have difficulty getting released from their identity.

In the Third Act this is made clear in the fate of Emily. Here for the first time in one of his dramas Wilder treats the question of the return of the dead to earth. Emily is present at her own burial and speaks with the deceased. She is still uneasy and nervous, in contrast to the other dead, who have a large measure of poise and detachment: "The dead sit in a quiet without stiffness, and in a patience without listlessness," [17] so the stage directions tells us at the outset. Mother Gibbs must admonish Emily: "Just wait and be patient." [18] Even though the dead have not yet by any means lost their identity, they have nonetheless gained great peace. But they still have interest in some things, whether by way of liking or dislike. One of them likes to hear church hymns, and Mrs. Soames, who sees a stunt in all familiar events, still shows some cheerful receptiveness when familiar occasions present themselves, the burial not excluded.

Emily now already begins to realize something: "I never realized before how troubled and how . . . how in the dark live persons are." [19] Living people's inability to see has already become clear to her, but—despite the dead Mrs. Gibbs' warnings—Emily has not yet gained patience and detachment enough to be able to renounce life entirely. She expects a festive day of life to give human warmth and great earthly radiance. Deep familiarity with the happy everyday things and the expectation of great sympathetic and consuming human love make a return to her former life seem urgently desirable to her. She is forced to recognize that absorption in everyday cares do not allow man to share in true living.

Emily's conclusion from a renewed earthly experience is: "That's all human beings are!—Just blind people. . . . That's what it was to be alive. To move about in a cloud of ignorance; to go up and down trampling on the feelings of those . . . of those about you. To spend and waste time as though you had a million years. To be always at the mercy of one self-centered passion, or another," adds Simon Stimson.[20]

Her earlier question to the stage manager was: "Do any human beings ever realize life while they live it?—every, every minute?" The answer of the stage manager is almost completely negative: "No.—The saints and poets, maybe— they do some." What the poets had to say is—leaving aside everything that is purely poetic and consequently of value by reason of its beauty of expression, and considering what they say purely as a metaphysical utterance—not very much. But they are in a position to grasp the brevity and the wonder of life, and possibly to portray the intensity of relations between humans, as well as the joy in the reflected splendor of earthly life.

Wilder develops in this play still another of his leading thoughts, namely, that the idea of the eternal is specifically linked to man. In the explanatory and introductory remarks to the Third Act the stage manager gives expression to this idea. He refers expressly to the fact that people already knew this truth. But out of a kind of pedagogic necessity, because people do not come very often to grips with this truth, he mentions it again: "I don't care what they say with their mouth—everybody knows that something is eternal. And it ain't houses, and it ain't names, and it ain't earth, and it ain't even the stars . . . everybody knows in their bones that something is eternal, and that something has to do with human beings . . . There's something way down deep that's eternal about every human being." [21] The eternal, which reaches still farther than the visible star—which Wilder so often evokes as a beacon and mainstay in the course of earthly life, and which even appears in the memories of dead people—can be gained only through the loss of identity, through distance, through separation from unrest:

"They're waitin'. They're waitin' for something that they feel is comin'. Something important and great. Aren't they waitin' for the eternal part in them to come out clear?" [22] In relation to the metaphysical posing of the problem and the shaping of it, the question of whence the impulse for this could have come is not so excessively important. The question is not of great significance whether Wilder's reflections began with Lucian's *Dialogues of the Dead* or with Edgar Lee Masters' *Spoon River Anthology*. More important is that from here there is a connection to the anthropological-archetypical play which Wilder especially intended.

The archetype is in portrayal always burdened with identity, but this identity does not threaten to splinter into mere individuality, but rather is centered upon a real complex of qualities and problems. With the archetype, literature becomes very restricted in its possibilities. It can no longer live from the interplay of the great diversities or maintain its existence largely from categories of the merely interesting. Where there is something like multiplicity (a play like *Our Town* suggests) it is only apparent, yet it is to be traced back to the great basic idea of constant recurrences.

Such a dramatic technique as this, however, cannot be worked endlessly without the public's becoming fatigued. This is especially the case when behind the dramatic anthropology and the concept of archetypes there stands a metaphysic that is modest and reserved in its answers and, at least in the field of cognition, gives no more than its exponents could often declare on the basis of rational reflection. Wilder seems to have realized this, for in his great world spectacle *The Skin of Our Teeth* to some extent he went in other directions and sought a longer perspective.

‹ 7 ›

The Skin of Our Teeth

ON OCTOBER 15, 1942, in the little Shubert Theater in New Haven, Connecticut, *The Skin of Our Teeth* received its first performance. This out-of-town premiere was followed on November 18 by the New York opening at the Plymouth Theater. Wilder's new play—with its title indicating alarm, hope, and resignation—was an outgrowth of world events and literary experiences since his last work. The Second World War had entered its fourth year, and for almost a year America had been actively engaged. Wilder does not pose any specifically political questions concerning this war, but directs his attention once again to the anthropological-ethical problem connected with it: If man survives this war too, will he fundamentally change his ways? There were many political programs during this war, but Wilder had experienced too much disillusionment after World War One—when he was already at the age of awareness—for him to place very much credence in the new program; and he had too clear an idea of man's limited possibilities and the chance of relapse to be able to share the renewed easy optimism. Antrobus speaks of all this in down-to-earth language in Act Three: "When you're at war you think about a better life; when you're at peace you think about a more comfortable one." [1] With all their stress on "reality," the politicians were bound to build their grand designs in a vacuum, because they did not take into account the really decisive thing, the world's anthropological substructure.

The literary problem of *The Skin of Our Teeth* was defined in a continuance of the dissolution of form, already suggested in *Our Town,* and now greatly radicalized with the introduction of anachronism, though not to the point of complete dissolution. At the end of the thirties Wilder had been intensely occupied with James Joyce, whose influence was to appear clearly in the multiple symbolism of *The Skin of Our Teeth,* and which led to not always gratifying disputes in American literary magazines. [2]

Viewed in relation to previous drama, the Wilder play differs in the manner of its division into three acts, and in a way also in the kind of plot as given by the title. The title implies that man once again escapes from his current plight and that his personal behavior approximates that of characters in a comedy—a comedy, to be sure, with metaphysical overtones rather than a straight comedy of definite time and place.

The play's three acts do not represent one continuous action. Each culminates in a great world catastrophe: the Ice Age, the Deluge, and the World War. Out of each catastrophe man finds his way by dint of his enthusiasm for a new beginning, without fundamentally changing his ways, for the evil which drove him into the catastrophe remains immanent in him.

Thus man is seen under two aspects: as a creature who is delivered up to these catastrophes, and as a creature who lives in the self-contained unit of the family. Wilder sets forth both of these aspects at the very beginning. In place of the usual prologue there are lantern-slide showings by the announcer, which are meant to give a graphic idea of the oppressive cold. This "prelude" alludes at the same time to the crisis within the family: a wedding ring is found with the inscription, "To Eve from Adam." [3]

From these lantern-slide showings Wilder shifts to the Antrobus family, which has to cope with the threatening Ice Age. It is a deranged and topsy-turvy world that is presented to us. In the warmest month, August, the severest frost prevails. The walls of the house rise, sink, and lean to one side. The dinosaur lives with man, at one point drolly taking its place with Mrs. Antrobus and the children in a triangular tableau reminiscent of Raphael. The alphabet is invented, and the fact is announced by telegram. Antrobus discovers the arithmetic significance of tens, though the course of the proceedings shows that the concept has long been part of the currency of human thought. Instability appears to be raised to the level of a principle, and anachronism displaces the normal time pattern.

There is plenty of fun with this hyper-baroque theater. Many over-serious playgoers, on the other hand, have been irritated by such "nonsense." The sense of what Wilder is up to is disclosed only when it is remembered that the real world of our life in the here-and-now was strongly called into question: the reality of this world had proved to be only a seeming reality.

All limited space is unreal—this is what had been shown by that whimsical address in *Our Town* which made reference to God as the ultimate reality in the universe:

REBECCA: It said: Jane Crofut; The Crofut Farm; Grover's Corners; Sutton County; New Hampshire; United States of America.

GEORGE: What's funny about that?

REBECCA: But listen, it's not finished: The United States of America; Continent of North America; Western Hemisphere; the Earth; the Solar System; the Universe; the Mind of God. . . .[4]

In our everyday life we are not in a position to penetrate the sense-deception of the world around us. Wilder returns to this idea, in the course of representing each hour of the twenty-four with a philosopher, at the ninth hour in the evening, represented by Spinoza:

> After experience had taught me that the common occurences of daily life are vain and futile; and I saw that all the objects of my desire and fear were in themselves nothing good nor bad save insofar as the mind was affected by them; I at length determined to search out whether there was something truly good and communicable to man.[5]

Spinoza with nine o'clock represents the beginning of the intellectually reflective hours of the night. Before being followed by Plato and Aristotle, he called attention to the meaning of the "common occurrences of daily life." But what a role these "common occurrences" have played in Wilder's dramas! *Our Town* was completely geared to them —only to lead them finally *ad absurdum* in the life of Emily. Seen from this standpoint, then, *The Skin of Our Teeth* is a consistent continuation of the small-town play. Of course it does not begin with the "occurrences," not even when in the course of the First Act the view narrows from the wide-angle lens of the "announcer" down to the family circle.

This Antrobus family lives in a dual system of categories, the one being in terms of nature and natural catastrophe, and the other being religious-eschatological. The name Antrobus is itself a hint of this; one thinks of the Greek word *anthropos*. Wilder represents him as the Chief of the mammals and president of their assembly. Antrobus speaks of the beginning of life billions of years ago, and he even gives a presentation of the polygenetic development of man.

But beside this there is another family tree and another chronology: here the span is not billions of years, but the 4,000 to 5,000 years of world history according to Biblical tradition. In this family tree, Antrobus becomes the Old Testament Adam, both figures merging to form a composite. From the statement of the "announcer," the provenance of Anthropos-Adam is clear: "He comes of very old stock and made his way up from next to nothing." Following Genesis, the "announcer" continues: "It is reported that he was once a gardener, but left that situation under circumstances that have been variously reported." [6] Antrobus is the genius who invented such things as the wheel (which is not expressly mentioned in the Bible); but he is also the inventor of beer, and this suggests the Biblical parallel Noah.

This parallel becomes still clearer with the events of the Second Act. When the Deluge comes, Antrobus takes pairs of all species of animal aboard the Ark, two by two, and thus helps to save creation. All animals are represented, even the famous Biblical snake to which Gladys calls attention while embarking.

The Biblical parentage is not limited to one meaning or one person, but, just as the natural racial parentage reflected all vital stages of development, so also the religious parentage has—if not all—many essential features in itself. Among these is the wounding of Antrobus that causes his limp: it is the wound he received in the fight over the absolute, the wound of Jacob. Sabina at one point characterizes him with mingled mockery and approval: ". . . An excellent husband and father, a pillar of the church, and has all the best interests of the community at heart. Of course, every muscle goes tight every time he passes a policeman." [7]

All this sounds very bourgeois, but the analogies point beyond: Antrobus is not only the first man, Adam, but also the progenitor of the people and guardian of the community, Abraham. The Biblical analogy probably extends to David, whose sins of the flesh are reflected in Antrobus. It is interesting to see how the analogy is not always unequivocal. The Henry-Cain analogy is an example: Cain has killed someone with a slingshot, the typical weapon of David.

Wilder has discussed at length the use of this kind of literatary technique in his lecture, "Goethe and World Literature." Referring to Goethe's thesis that "national literature" now does not "say" much and that one must take into account mankind's "long memory"—Wilder is borrowing a phrase from Ortega y Gasset—Wilder takes up the subject of Goethe's employment of universal materials: "He did not shrink from anachronisms. He wedded his Faust to Helena; he grafted his Weimar on to Shiraz, the city of the Persian poet." [8] It is not a question here of whether the examples Wilder has chosen from Goethe are, from the standpoint of tradition, entirely correct. What is much more important in the present connection is Wilder's reference to Goethe's mode of relating and integrating things of different cultures. The character of national literature as such is not obliterated: "Only the relation between the things themselves (as it exists in our mind) becomes altered, and in view of such alteration he asserts that national literature no longer says much." [9]

To illustrate his own procedure, Wilder might also have adduced the Goethean concept of "supplementation." When Goethe asserts that the mythological ideas of the ancients must be "supplemented," he is alluding to those complements and those bridges of the imagination which are to Wilder by no means unfamiliar.[10]

The recourse to world literature is important for Wilder in another sense also. He sees in it the expression of the fact that man as an individual is in the millions—a view that may also have its significance in connection with his speculations about the soul's divestment of its individuality after death.

A rather casual remark in *The Merchant of Yonkers* is an indication of this: "Oh, I used to say that people were meant to go through life two by two. But the older I grow I say—four by four—hundred by hundred—thousand by thousand—million by million." [11]

And in Wilder's essay on Goethe there is this: "With all its xenophobia, the Old Testament is superabundant in consciousness of man as a countless number and of time as immensity." [12] The sense for this is given only by the inclusion of the thought of ruin and death, and especially the countless numbers of the dead. Immensity signifies the huge number of the dead in which the individual disappears. The primeval human types also lived in the immensity of the Old Testament.

From the beginning it is quite definite that Henry is Cain. Sabina gives it away at the beginning of the First Act. A tactful yet incautious question by Moses awakens Mrs. Antrobus' grief over the loss of Abel. It is she who tries again and again with her apron to rub away the mark of Cain from her son's forehead—but it remains. Cain, too, must remain. From a dramaturgic standpoint he is the recurrent type; from a metaphysical standpoint he is the Evil that must accompany man. His existence makes Antrobus despair and wish himself rid of this son who makes himself intolerable in all polite society. Evil is ordained for him as the curse of man's original Fall. Nor can it be domesticated. Wilder has included in *The Skin of Our Teeth* a number of contrast scenes by which he aims to show that man in a state of peril gives himself up to illusions. Thus we see Sabina in bourgeois fashion doing the housework and dusting everything when the Ice Age is already close at hand. Thus we see Antrobus just before the Flood, planning to take his sweetheart to a hotel room. Above all there is the scene in which Antrobus, who should have no illusions about Cain's nature, sits at the family hearth drilling him in the multiplication table.

The essential element is the constant accompaniment of that which is evil, with which Antrobus must identify himself, as in the scene where Sabina breaks the news to him that Cain has killed the neighbors' son. At first Antrobus is extremely angry, and despite the approach of the Ice Age he wants to stamp out the life-preserving fire—on which everything constantly depends and which only Mrs. Antrobus is really competent to preserve—and in this way to put an end to everything. Then the sense of his own guilt returns: "Henry! Henry! (Puts his hand on his forehead.) Myself. All of us, we're covered with blood." [13]

But Antrobus seeks again to evade this recognition of complicity with evil. In the Second Act a Negro is not safe from the assaults of Henry-Cain. When he "wounds" him and Antrobus learns of it, he tries to withdraw from the affair with the words of Pilate, "I wash my hands . . ." That is an exculpation not only in the eschatological realm, but also in terms of the plot of the Second Act. At the beginning of Act Two, Antrobus had reached the crest of a wave, and had issued the slogan, "Enjoy yourself." His wife, on the other hand, realizing the internal threat to the family, had sounded the call to "save the family." When Cain wants to kill the Negro, he offers as his excuse: "All I wanted to do was—have some fun," [14] which recalls his father's slogan at the beginning of the act.

Antrobus is the master of the house, who should give the family its solidarity, whereas Cain is increasingly the one without any ties, who wants no home and no solidarity. Even a total war with all its consequences cannot awake such desires in him. When Henry-Cain after the world war emerges a general from the air raid shelter, he rejects all shelter and all ties, to say nothing of order and subordination. His mother's wish that there be peace at last in the family as well as in the world, he brusquely rejects: "I don't live here. I don't belong to anybody." [15]

Still stronger is his negation of his father: "You don't have to think I'm any relation of yours. I haven't got any father or any mother, or brothers or sisters. And I don't want any. And what's more I haven't got anybody over me; and I never will have. I'm alone, and that's all I want to be: alone." [16] The man without any ties, the man who denies, is also the man who brooks no commandments: "Nobody can say *must* to me." [17]

Henry-Cain is also the embodiment of the so-called new political principles, which equate youth with an unbridled striving for power. All contemporaries still remember the words, "What have they done for us?", and still more "When are you going to wake up?" [18] Toward the play's end, however, Wilder does not see Cain as representing the revolt of youth, but as a representation of strong unreconciled evil, of whom it is said in the stage directions at the very end: "Henry appears at the edge of the scene, brooding and unreconciled, but present." [19] When creation begins again, he is there, just as at the second Creation by Noah the serpent was also among those present.

Among the female characters Mrs. Antrobus is Eve (Hebrew for "the maternal one") who guards the fire that keeps life. Opposed to her is Sabina as the other Eve, the temptress. Sabina appears in the play under various names which give clues to her identity. When the characters are introduced by the announcer, she is called Lily Sabina; she is also called the servant girl.[20] She is the daughter of Lilith of Talmudic tradition; and Lilith is of the night, demonic: she is the evil female, the night-hag.

She has not come into the family by orderly process, but—as her name Sabina indicates—by rapine. In the first argument between the two main female characters of the play, Mrs. Antrobus gives the facts about Sabina's past: "O, Sabina, I know you. When Mr. Antrobus raped you home from your Sabine hills, he did it to insult me. You were the new wife, weren't you?" [21] But Sabina finally did not hold her place. She let the fire go out, and was demoted to the kitchen to be servant instead of guardian of the fire. In the next-to-last scene of the Third Act she says resignedly: "Kitchen! Why is it that however far I go away, I always find myself back in the kitchen?" [22] For her, life has no other final solution than servitude.

In the Second Act it does appear for a time that her hour has come. Her name is enlarged to Sabina Fairweather, a reference to the time of her effectiveness. In crises she always fails; in fair weather she is able to achieve recognition, as when Antrobus becomes President. But it is President of a state full of illusions, where the "truth" is obtained from the fortune-teller and accomplice of prostitutes. Esmeralda the gypsy seems to have the power of regulating the action, but it is action that is altogether brittle and cannot last. The brief dream of Helen of Troy, about whom Sabina asks the fortune-teller, is finally over, and Sabina says naïvely: "I don't know why my life's always being interrupted—just when everything's going fine!" [23] Esmeralda has just banished her to the kitchen: "Yes, go—back to the kitchen with you." [24]

The Second Act not only marks Sabina's seduction of Mr. Antrobus and demonstrates his moral blindness in seeing in the prostitute the loved one; but also, in the Second Act, it is through Sabina that Antrobus becomes conscious of his own guilt. When he sees Gladys wearing the red stockings, the color of Man's Fall and of temptation, he realizes at once that the source of this is Sabina. His own guilt causes him to guard against his daughter's going wrong.

The four main characters—Mr. and Mrs. Antrobus, Henry, and Sabina—make up the world, in its good aspect as well as its bad. The one cannot be divorced from the other, and nothing can be made an absolute value. The human archetypes which these characters embody form the foundation on which being—for Wilder, Christian being—rests. In them Wilder's cycle of theological existence runs a full course: "The Fall as the result of sin, the dawning consciousness of what is sinful, the new beginning in excessive hope and in pride, and thereby the first beginning of a new Fall."

Viewing these archetypes simplifies one's perception of the world, and Wilder does this consciously in order to avoid diffusion and confusion. This does not mean, however, that he has purposely renounced all additional characters, for the dramatis personae of *The Skin of Our Teeth* is fairly extensive. But either they are little more than walk-on roles or they are auxiliary roles, and are meant to elucidate the archetypes or what the archtypes personify.

We have already discussed the nature of the anachronistic characters. Not mentioned in that connection were Moses, Homer, and the Muses, as well as the great philosophers who play such an important role in the Third Act. For Antrobus the great books are expressions of the great tradition of world thought, and as such are unquestionably of great significance. As the Ice Age approaches, Mrs. Antrobus is supposed to burn all the books except Shakespeare. She finds this ridiculous, because she would not spare Shakespeare if it prevented her from keeping one of her children from catching cold.

On the question of whom to save from the encroaching ice, Antrobus is for taking in all those whom Mrs. Antrobus regards as unnecessary mouths to feed in this emergency. But Antrobus intervenes decisively in behalf of the man who makes all laws, Moses. To Antrobus, pulling through means not just the physical preservation of the human species: "And if the ice melts? . . . And if we pull through? Have you and I been able to bring up Henry? What have we done?" [25]

It is less easy to save Homer and the Muses. Antrobus does not even trouble them to take over Henry's education. Henry's problem—in the realm of the archetypical—is not one of cultural education. In the scene in Act One where Antrobus cuffs Henry while drilling him in the multiplication table, there is here—as we have already seen—the resuming of a domestic scene, an illustration of man's tendency to lull himself into a feeling of security in the midst of a threatened world.

Important as Shakespeare, Homer, and the Muses are for Antrobus, still more important now are Moses and, above all, the books of the philosophers. They are the "voices to guide us." [26] God has given us the philosophers so that we may obtain guidance from their books. The practice of philosophy has not come of its own power but through God's grace.

Through the philosophers man receives clarity: through Spinoza (ninth hour), who warns of the confusion of the external world, and Plato (tenth hour) who warns of confusion within, and Aristotle who praises the state of reason in which the object is comprehended with energy, a state that is granted to man only at times but which God always possesses (eleventh hour). Philosophy lasts until the twelfth hour, when the Bible resumes its sway with the beginning of Genesis.

This last is an indication of the coincidence of the beginning and the end, the Alpha and Omega of Christianity.

With the alphabet, as we have seen, the circumstances vary in the play. Antrobus is supposed to have invented it, but at a critical point he attributes the invention to Moses. It is the subject of human instruction and the criterion of intel ligence and ability for the rising generation; thus it is said jocosely of Cain that he would pass a test if only the alphabet could first be simplified.

In addition to all these utterances is one that Sabina occasionally makes: "Why, when the alphabet's finished we'll be able to tell the future and everything." [27] This sounds very naïve coming from Sabina, who like Mrs. Antrobus does not know the first thing about the alphabet, or from Cain, who cannot quite master it. But behind her naïveté is an utterance that, though in one sense evidencing Sabina's naïve belief in progress, at a deeper level has another meaning. It is that when the prophecies of the Bible are all fulfilled, time is then fulfilled, Revelation is clear, and there are no longer any mysteries.[28]

Wilder's Christian humanism appears very clearly in this passage. The constant recurrences of extreme crisis, the perpetual accompaniment by evil, personified by Cain—the entire plot structure of *The Skin of Our Teeth* can give rise to the thought that man is in a vicious circle. But there are clear signs that Wilder did not mean the play to be so interpreted. Man has the faculty of memory, which, though it does not keep him from getting into a critical or threaten- ing situation, does prevent him from being actually steered into a vicious circle.

Besides his memory, his constancy, and his passion—at time illusionist—or resurgence, the thing that above all maintains man is the voices of the philosophers. The voices supply the unconditioned frame of reference for man's reflection. Making reference to them need not necessarily be understood as the mark of the "educated" person. Wilder illustrates this with a stage trick that at first is irritating. An announcement is made that the players have fallen ill and are being replaced by the simplest kind of emergency substitutes, such as the wardrobe mistress and others. These can bring the voices of the philosophers to the people in the very same way as can the major actors of the play or the leaders of the intellectual world. One's first reaction is that the stage help is actually being called on to meet an emergency; but in the metaphysical sphere, which is the goal of Wilder's efforts, the situation attains human universality.

The normal solid surface of theatrical presentation is nowhere to be seen in this play. In *Our Town*, the scope was the family circle and the task of the stage manager was to seek reality outside narrow confines or to transfer it there. *The Skin of Our Teeth*, on the other hand, has all areas for its sphere. The mythic accord is effected by means of the aforementioned anachronisms. We get an idea of each and all of them, in order to become clear in our minds that the world which surrounds us does not have that reality which we concede it.

Translated into the language of the theater, this is still another way of saying that the box-set stage has given us a false picture of the world. What is needed is to vanquish the box-set stage, if one wishes to banish, first, the false notion of the realities tied to little details of the scenery, and secondly, a linear sense of time. In the kind of theater that Wilder has in mind here, there would also be no separation of public and stage. In the Second Act there is only a seeming contradiction of this, for the audience in the ocean and the players on the beach are both acting amid scenery that is about to change.

In this play Sabina is the one to whom Wilder assigns the task of establishing the link with "reality," as that term is understood by people generally. She repeatedly acts out of character. She does not understand the play or does not want to. Parts of it she does not want to play because a friend of hers is present in the theater and parts of it might shock her by recalling her own hard fate.

But Sabina's function is also that she must ironically play the play out. At one point she names the play by its title. As Miss Somerset, she says three times in the First Act: ". . . A few years ago we came through the depression by the skin of our teeth! One more tight squeeze like that and where will we be?" [29] The audience receives a strong and sustained statement of the play's theme, but the words are in an ironical context, for this very statement is also a cue line and the prompter is unable to respond. Miss Somerset makes use of the breakdown to address herself to the audience.

Through her outbursts she establishes the link to the audience, and the stage manager has to bring her back into the action of the play. Thus the stage manager has a function somewhat the reverse of that in *Our Town*. In that play, within his technical limits, he let the people come forward; and he repeatedly bridged the gap between the transcendental area and the here-and-now. In *The Skin of Our Teeth* the transcendental is itself here, and the task of the stage manager is limited.

The startling effects are so increased in *The Skin of Our Teeth* that they bear upon the movement and the success of the play itself. Occasionally a minor character such as the telegraph boy makes a remark to this effect: "I . . . I can't do this last part very well." [30] Antrobus too has trouble with his role. In a scene in which Sabina has created a sort of general chaos, he cannot get back on the track right away. Antrobus: "Wait a minute. I can't get back into it as easily as all that." [31]

Sabina is the one who, more than anyone else, puts

everything in question. She seems to have certain intellectual difficulties. When it dawns on her that the crisis also brings the refugee problem, she briefly gives vent to her feelings. She tries to avert an ugly encounter between the angry father and the furious son by saying: "Stop! Stop! Don't play this scene," [32] even reminding the players what happened when this scene was played in the previous evening's performance.

Sabina, the frivolous one, who in *The Skin of Our Teeth* does not see any eschatological event but only sees a threat, gives vent to her aversion to the play: "I hate this play and every word in it. As for me, I don't understand a single word of it, anyway—all about the troubles the human race has gone through, there's a subject for you." [33]

Wilder even takes the opportunity to have Sabina make sarcastic remarks about him as a dramatist. Sabina, in a Commedia dell' Arte situation, had been told by the prompter to improvise something, at which she had only poor success. She now gives her opinion of the play's content, which is unclear and seems to have been insufficiently thought out: "Besides the author hasn't made up his silly mind as to whether we're all living back in caves or in New Jersey today, and that's the way it is all the way through." [34]

Something of their double nature is still to be detected in the characters, their ephemeral quality bound by time and place, as well as their human universality. In the inclinations of the characters there is still the father-daughter and mother-son relationship—Maggie is concerned for Henry, Antrobus for Gladys—just as in *Our Town*. But by making the usual space and time relationships questionable from the beginning, Wilder manages to reach the sphere that encompasses the millions of living and dead. The play's entire design in this respect is anchored so firmly in the typological that in the nomenclature of persons as well as places there is a visible trend to universality, to the meta-physical comedy of types, and to the grand style.

In *The Skin of Our Teeth* there is no longer a Grover's Corners that can be located by its degree of latitude and longitude, no Webbs and no Gibbses, but only the four basic human types, who are, to be sure, organized as a family, but whose significance is purely archetypical. Even when specific place names are still given, as in the brief listing of school, department store, etc., they are not meant to play any role in the play, but represent certain human necessities: education, divine worship, satisfaction of one's daily wants. They will remain, according to Wilder's view, as will also the primeval types of good and evil in a world of recurring catastrophes. "Oh, anyway," Sabina exclaims, "nothing matters! It'll all be the same in a hundred years." [35] It is Sabina, too, who closes the play, shuffling the levels of reality as she refers simultaneously to herself, the audience, and humanity: "This is where you came in. We have to go on for ages and ages yet." [36]

≺ 8 ≻

Short Plays

WILDER'S short plays—some of them written when he was teaching in college—all come in the early part of his career, and, in any chronological study of his dramas, would have to be examined at the beginning. In the context of his total output, however, they are often of such small importance—especially in content—that it would clog one's approach to the weightier matter in his later dramas were one to assign these short plays much space at the outset.

Wilder regarded them as experimental in nature. He tried in them a number of dramatic devices, some of which were to find larger application in his later plays. We have already seen these devices at work in this latter context; let us now turn back to look at them in their original form.

Our remarks, of course, cannot be limited solely to these technical devices. For even in the "three-minute plays" and the short dramas a religious problem is already being raised which, though showing the influence of youthful religious zeal and the resort to paradox, also reveals features that, in their wholly unorthodox way, already tend toward laying a new foundation of faith.

The religious drama, which Wilder is striving to institute in these plays, and which—as he emphasizes in the Preface to *The Angel That Troubled the Waters, and Other Plays*—is intended as evidence that its author is "not only as gentle as doves, but as wise as serpents," [1] is, even in content, written with the aim of touching the audience once again, of meeting it in a sphere beyond the mere "good manners" of standard religious sentiment.

This does not mean coarseness, nor does it even mean originality at any price, as many Europeans would be only too glad to assume. Nor does it lead to dramatic exaggerations aimed at bestirring the audience by means of some catastrophe. Wilder's prime consideration in his early plays is conditioned by the genus of the drama and its stage possibilities.

For the modern dramatist, creative technique is not only a matter of pure experiment, but also an instrument for voicing his world philosophy. The conventional stage is for him a hindrance that he must overcome. We have already analyzed Wilder's attempts to do this in *Our Town* and *The Skin of Our Teeth*. Among the short dramas there is also a work that is especially aimed to serve this end: *Proserpina and the Devil*. It is a puppet-play, but not consistently so. The only characters that really engage in dialogue are those who put on the play, namely the theater manager and two puppet operators. The puppets themselves act in a dumb-show instead of being given the usual ventriloquist voices.

Wilder had given his play two strands of plot: the play of the puppets, about which we are oriented by the stage directions, and the excited dialogue of the puppet operators, who argue about the blunders in the play and create considerable disillusion in the audience.

The play's inner continuity, thus interrupted, is brought further to dissolution by the fact that the various figures are taken from widely different periods of history: Abraham,

Penelope and Jephtha's daughter, Midas and Harlequin, Proserpina and Pluto, the last-named acting in the form of a medieval Satan. All this seems like pell-mell disorder, and the confusion is further accented as Noah's Ark raises a mute protest against the miscarried action on the stage and Styx and Acheron are replaced with circular cloths in the stage decor.

Many of the ideas of the later Wilder—for example, the idea that there is an affinity and occasionally also an inner continuity between figures of religion and mythology—seem to be already hinted at here. Thus the Pluto of antiquity finds his continuation in the medieval Satan, and Styx and Acheron become the Lake of Wrath of the Bible. From this turmoil one can also discern the theme of Adam and Eve's Original Sin: Proserpina's spouse, who represents Satan, persuades her to eat the apple (here it is an orange). "With an odd recollection of the Garden of Eden, she tempts him into eating the remaining half." [2]

The parallel drawn between Proserpina and Eve is not so arbitrary as it might at first appear. Proserpina, according to the ancient myth, had eaten of the pomegranate, symbol of fertility, and was thereby "wedded" to Pluto. Thus there had been a kind of "Original Sin."

In the tumult and confusion arising from the actors' inability to master the characters after their director has gone into a tavern, it is difficult to find a continuing thread of plot and to find one's bearings on the two levels of action. But the turbulence produced in the play is above all to be interpreted as a protest against the box-set stage, with its separation of author, players, and audience, and the seemingly logical and firm thread of its plot, which is spun at a distance.

If this play has a meaning in terms of the religious teaching intended by Wilder, it is that when the great stage manager abandons his authority, the most corrupt figures take control and govern without hindrance, and the results are chaotic or even pernicious.

The three-minute play at the same time raises the following basic question which is linked to Wilder's dramatic production: "Where actually is reality to be found?" Not in so-called "realistic" representation, which gives little or no scope to thought, nor in the sort of thinking manifested in the customary dramatic models that make a conventional arrangement of time and space. Such thinking, like the old-style stage, offers the playgoer a hastily produced sense of reality.

But what is reality, and what leads to reality? Wilder, as almost all his plays show, places special value upon grasp of reality and its dramatic reproduction. In *Mozart and the Grey Steward* there is a passage which is a key to evaluating critical realism. The Grey Steward says to Mozart who is already in the shadow of death: "Know first that all the combinations of circumstance can suffer two interpretations, the apparent and the real." [3]

The term "combination of circumstance" could refer to the psychological degree of probability of the characters' actions; but, as Wilder's short plays show, what is meant is a plot construct which leads into the regions of metaphysics. The combination of characters is alone sufficient indication of this. The series of short plays commences with *Nascuntur Poetae*. It is possibly an allusion to a passage in Cicero's *De Oratore,* or a modification of Sir Philip Sidney's saying, *Orator fit, poeta nascitur.* The description given at the beginning as part of the stage directions relates to a painting by Piero di Cosimo, in which the persons come together for a dramatic discussion. This idea in drama is not entirely new: As so-called vivification of the portrait, use has been made of it repeatedly, as it also has been for vivification of a group portrait.[4] But in this play of Wilder's we are not concerned with a group of real-life persons, but with two allegorical figures: the Woman in the Chlamys and the Woman in Deep Red. To these two there is opposed, at all events, a real-life figure, that of the incipient poet.

The combination of real-life and otherworldly figures is also characteristic of most of Wilder's other short plays. One of several examples is *Childe Roland to the Dark Tower Came.* (The title possibly is taken from *King Lear,*[5] in which Edgar speaks a three-line verse of an old Scottish ballad of which various features and details are borrowed from the Legend of Charlemagne.) To "The Girl" and "The Dark Girl" in the Tower of Death in this play, there is opposed a figure of earthly legend. The same feature appears still more distinctly in *Hast Thou Considered My Servant Job?,* in which Satan and Christ argue over the soul of Judas; here the theme is taken from the Book of Job. In *Leviathan,* two figures of mythology stand in opposition to a deceased prince. *And the Sea Shall Give Up Its Dead,* the title of which is also taken from the Bible,[6] has to do with the process of divestment of self by three deceased persons. In *Now the Servant's Name Was Malchus,* the story of Malchus in the Bible is thoroughly discussed between Jesus and Malchus. In most of these plays—and also in the short dramas that do not treat of specifically metaphysical questions—a trinity of characters predominates. There is some likelihood that the three-minute play had the three-person play for a model. Much more likely, however, is that the trinity was retained for intrinsic dramatic reasons: a large number of characters could hardly find place in a short play such as this without bursting its confines, and two characters alone would too easily give to the play the quality of a mere discussion piece.

From the preponderance of metaphysical or quasi-metaphysical characters it can be seen, however, where in these plays the center of Wilder's interest in reality actually lies. In addition, in some of Wilder's short dramas the way between the here-and-now and the hereafter, as well as some related ideas, has been given, if not a thorough examination, at least the hint of a study within the exceedingly short span of the plot.

The choice of characters has otherworldly overtones. In six of the short plays the locus of the action is unreal by ordinary standards of reality. The six are *Childe Roland to the Dark Tower Came, And the Sea Shall Give Up Its Dead, Has Thou Considered My Servant Job?, The Angel That Troubled the Waters, Leviathan,* and in a way *Nascuntur Poetae.* In this last, to be sure, the young poet emerges from a figurative, prefigured status into the world of human life; but the road that seems destined for him leads through earthly hardship to a perfection that has been prescribed for him.

That this is a metaphysical play is intimated not only by the plot's directed quality, the locale, and the constellation of characters, but also by the plot *per se,* which hardly exists in the sense of a plot of the old-style drama. This last is of course partly due to the shortness of these plays, but the fact is also that the directed quality of the characters excludes any conflict from the plot. There is a resistance against the strange knowledge and the strange sphere of being that lies enclosed in death. A favorite theme in Wilder is the aversion, even after death, to the loss of individual identity. There is fear of the plague and fear of suffering, but there cannot be a struggle against the unalterable demand of the other world. This means that a true dramatic conflict in these plays is largely eliminated.

The unusualness of these plays also appears in their stage directions, which often far exceed what is customary.

That the short play requires more detailed stage directions than the full-length drama is by no means the only reason, much less the decisive one, for these directions underline strongly the unusual character of the scenery of these plays.

In *Childe Roland to the Dark Tower Came* the landscape itself plays a role, as we see from the stage directions: "The knight blows his horn; the landscape collects itself to listen. . . . The landscape laughs, then falls suddenly silent. . . . The marsh becomes animated and fully interested in the stranger." [7]

If it is a fact that Wilder's initial inspiration for this play came from Browning's poem of the same title, this inspiration may also have included the anthropomorphosis of the landscape. Here are examples:

> Those two hills on the right,
> Crouched like two bulls locked horn in horn in fight;
> While to the left, a tall scalped mountain. . .
> Dunce,
> Dotard, a-dozing at the very nonce,
> After a life spent training for the sight!   (XXX)

And:

> The hills, like giants at a hunting, lay,
> Chin upon hand, to see the game at bay—   (XXXII)

By omitting the comparative "like," Wilder has carried the anthropomorphosis to an extreme length.

The play about Judas closes with this stage direction: "Suddenly the thirty pieces of silver are cast upward from the revolted hand of Judas. They hurtle through the skies, flinging their enormous shadows across the stars and continue falling for ever through the vast funnel of space." [8] This magical happening certainly goes even further than the landscape's participation in *Childe Roland*. Through supernatural forces the liquidation of the deed of one of the great culprits of Christian world history is undertaken, whereas in *Childe Roland* the landscape's participation in the action constitutes a kind of mimicry which accentuates the general effect.

Besides those stage directions which bear immediately upon the play's metaphysical endeavor, there are many others which describe either the gesture or even—as in *Leviathan*—the pantomime. They serve to disencumber the dialogue, or to emphasize certain ideas in the text without an undesirable increase in the text itself. This is, in a way, an exactly contrary example to Shakespeare, the length of whose dramas was such that he permitted himself descriptions of gestures as well as actions, probably because the poor lighting of the Elizabethan theater prevented some of the audience from following the players' gestures.

The metaphysics in the stage notes, as well as the references to actions required in the plot, lend to these short plays a character that lies beyond the usual ideas of the drama and its functions. Not everything is the outgrowth of a grand new design. Much is the more or less necessary result of the abbreviated form of such dramatic experiments; other things were influenced more by speculation as to the religious content, which adhered to individual features—sometimes extensive features—of Christian tradition, but which —as will be shown further on—had for its purpose the radical revival of domestic Christian faith. "The intermittent sincerity of generations of clergymen and teachers has rendered embarrassing and even ridiculous all the terms of the spiritual life." [9]

A play lasting only a few minutes naturally cannot have a genuine dramatic thread of plot. Nowhere in the "three-minute plays" is such a thing really to be found. In the specifically religious plays the problem, as we have suggested, is set in such a way that the force of an other-world power is too strong for a real dramatic conflict to take place. Malchus is disarmed by the Lord's great candor, Judas is gripped as by a supernatural power and throws away the thirty pieces of silver, which go flying through space. In *The Angel That Troubled the Waters,* which takes up the story of the Pool of Bethesda in St. John's Gospel,[10] the cure of a physical injury is brought about by supernatural power. But a paradox remains: spiritual illness cannot be healed, but by it man is placed in a position to exert power for the Lord: "Without your wound where would your power be? It is your very remorse that makes your low voice tremble into the hearts of men. The very angels themselves cannot persuade the wretched and blundering children on earth as can one human being broken in the wheels of living. In Love's service only the wounded soldiers can serve." [11] Such utterances lead the Christian's thoughts to the events in the life and work of Jesus and St. Paul.

But Wilder has also spoken these thoughts in the more mundane parts of the "three-minute plays": he has done this in those passages that have to do with the artist, also in *Nascuntur Poetae.* The impatience at delay at the beginning ("Why are we delaying?") and the presumptuous "I will astonish it," i.e., life (the words' especially intended effect being one of inversion, viz., that it is not life that will astonish *him*) —are followed by the appearance of a figure clothed in red, color of martyrdom. Through this figure there is set in motion the process of realization—so essential to the artist—that only by means of the dark and difficult impulses can the poet's calling be given its proper character.

Similar thoughts appear in Wilder's novels. Thus in *The Woman of Andros,* Chrysis embodies this idea, just as Alix does in *The Cabala.* In *The Bridge of San Luis Rey* the same thesis is brought out especially strongly, that suffering, unfulfilled desires, unrequited love, and loneliness are especially sound prerequisites for a life of service to man.

The theme is again taken up in *Mozart and the Grey Steward,* in which the purely temporal and here-and-now element of the plot is shunted aside by the Grey Steward, the messenger of death. He is already marked as such by symbolic attributes: gray color, the handkerchief that is meant to keep away the odor of decomposition, and the reference to the undertaker, here made with a touch of irony: "One would say, an elegant undertaker." [12]

As long as Mozart stands on the plane of visible everyday realities, his will is to refuse the messenger's request that he compose a requiem for Countess Walsegg, because he sees in this primarily an attempt by the Count to feed his own vanity by ascribing the authorship of the requiem to himself. Once he has been led to the deeper dilemmas of the world, however, Mozart gives up the egocentrism which had been expressed in his view that artists could create for themselves and had their gifts simply for their personal use. The more clearly aware Mozart becomes of his own nearness to death, the more he recognizes man's despair. He must give to the despairing ones a voice: "Only through the intercession of great love, and of great art, which is love, can that despairing cry be eased." [13]

Wilder in this play goes so far as to have Mozart regard Countess Walsegg's death as substituting for the death of the millions of deceased. Undignified in life, she becomes great through suffering and horrible death. Mozart kisses the adornments of the lowly ones. ". . . Only he who has kissed the leper can enter the kingdom of art." [14]

Brother Fire draws its subject matter from the life of Saint Francis, and in this play too the metaphysical element predominates. Francis calls the fire his brother and—a thought which Wilder pursues in *The Bridge of San Luis Rey*—fire and brother are interchangeable.

Wilder's thorough knowledge of the Bible leads him to the thought that fire is an element of divine wrath [15] or of damnation.[16] This view is excluded from the discussion: ". . . I know that there is flame to burn all evil in the Lake of the Damned. I do not speak of that now . . ." [17] But for Francis fire is of the essence in another sense: God can harbor and protect man in the midst of these elements, and the Biblical evidence for this is not only the story of the three young men in the fiery furnace, but also numerous other passages in the Old Testament, such as Numbers, Chapter 11, Verse 2; Psalm 56, Verse 12; and Isaiah, Chapter 43, Verse 2.

The blessed of the Lord can walk in fire: ". . . But I know also that fire is at all times useful to the great Blessed. It surrounds them and they dwell in it." [18] The typical naïve realist such as Mother Annunziata does not realize this significance of fire. Through Church tradition she hears of the Old Testament fire-sacrifice and its transformation into the new fire-sacrifice of love, but she is guided by a logic which is foreign to the religious person, and which cannot serve the ends of love.

The child faces the mystery of fire in another way. Recognizing fire's symbolic power, the child remains on the side of Brother Francis. When the child's mother forbids it to speak with the saint, a secret understanding develops between the two. They guard and tend the fire. They are at one in selfless love and can manage the flames of the fire as the dead can. To Annunziata's question as to where Saint Francis' mother is, the saint replies that she is in Heaven, where she feeds those flames that would have died out on earth.

If in these short plays the problem is predetermined by

the character types, the metaphysical preponderance is replaced by a more religious-psychological view. To this latter group of plays belongs *The Angel on the Ship*. Its opening scenes could easily be taken for idolatry. The crew of a ship that is in distress at sea takes the figurehead on the bow which they have known for thirty years and make it a god, pray to it and petition it for deliverance from distress.

The distress situation that leads to prayers is used by Wilder for purposes of a religious-psychological differentiation. Van turns to the divinity with primitive fanaticism, which is further accentuated by his Oriental attitude of prayer: "Great gawd Lily, on the ship 'Nancy Bray' all's lost with us if you don't bring us rain to drink. . . . Youm allus been the angel on the front of this yere ship 'Nancy Bray,' and you ain't goin to leave us rot now. I finished my prayer, great gawd Lily. Amen." [19] All qualities reminiscent of or required for Christian prayer are here left out of account. There is no gratitude for the care that has been taken of them up to now, no personal confession of guilt, and if there is any reverence at all toward the deity it is expressed at most in the attribute "great."

The prayer of the Captain's wife has another tone: "You knows everything, and you knows what I did to my husband and that I didn't let him have none of the secret water that me and Van saved up, and that when he died he knew it and cursed me and Van to hell. But youm forgiven everything, and send us some rain or by-and-by we'll die and there'll be no one here prayin' to you. This is the end of my prayin', great God Lily." [20]

This prayer at least asks pardon for a crime—of course, only for a crime which has led to the present critical situation. The misdeed itself, or her sinful life as such, play no part in the woman's prayer.

Sam's own prayer most approximates that which we

understand to be a Christian prayer. It has none of the
negative qualities we have noted in the prayer of Minna,
and, above all, it is free of the heavy stress on her own usefulness that tainted Minna's prayer:

> God forgive me, great God Lily, I'm old Jamaica Sam that don't
> never go ashore. Amen. I'd be drownd too, only for Van and
> the Captain's wife, who gave me some of the secret water, so that
> if they died I could roll 'em over the side and not leave 'em
> on the clean deck. Amen. Youm known my whole life, great God
> Lily, and how I stole the Portagee's red bag, only it was almost
> empty, and . . . and that other thing. Send a lot of rain and a
> ship to save us. Amen.[21]

The mixture of egoism and despair that an emergency
brings out reveals itself still more crassly in the further
course of the play. Van takes up the subject of the death of
the Captain, who was not allowed his fair share of the
drinking water; but he at once declares himself innocent,
and in the same breath lets it be known that more is at
stake for him than the saving of his own life, that there is
also an inheritance from a relative living in Amsterdam.—
Minna's conduct is governed entirely by her personal despair. In the threatening destruction she sees a punishment
for her crimes.

Their sudden rescue from this distress creates the play's
seeming paradox. Minna and Van immediately renounce
the heathen deity, while Sam—who came closest to the
manner of Christian prayer—wants to hold fast to it: "But
that's the great God Lily. Her's saved us. You ain't goin' to
do anything to her?" [22]

As Wilder sees it, the face value of Christianity is in a
bad way. In time of distress prayer is shortened and distorted. Whoever, like Sam, retains it in its Christian mode,
adheres to the idols of the time of distress. Religious fidelity

can lead to a paradox, but in paradox it can remain more pregnant with life than it can in another form. In presenting such a problem on the stage Wilder has removed himself far from revealed Christianity. The vexation caused him by a pagan world that is administered by Christian forms has led him to a religious experience that is founded merely on psychology.

The false starts in our Christian faith, which have arisen especially through the transfer of the thought of individuality—these, and the deficient constancy and the distortion of man in time of distress, find an extension in the falsely applied rationality which is treated in the typically Wilderian mystery play, *Flight Into Egypt*. It is a story that takes the Biblical material merely as a point of departure, in order to bring to bear, in drastic super-rationalistic manner, the religious lesson of Christianity.

The content of the play is as follows: Mary and Joseph, with the child Jesus, are on the flight into Egypt. The child is carried by a female donkey that is able to speak, and her speech is not merely imitative sounds, but the speech of reason. She is *rationis capax,* but out of this very faculty arise difficulties for her: She does not take into account the persecuted state of the three, and is less concerned with the danger than with her own fatigue.

She is willing to assume the task given her, but only within the limits of reason: "I'm willing to carry you as far and as fast as I can, but within reason." [23] When she is advised that she is carrying the Lord before Whom all had knelt in Bethlehem, she becomes more zealous for a time. Apparently she recognizes the primacy of the task of saving God above all rational speculation: "Lord, what a donkey I was to be arguing about reason while my Lord was in danger." [24] But again doubts arise, this time the fear of crocodiles, a fear that evidently seems more important than the history-making task that has been assigned to her. What Wilder is getting at here is rational discussion of religious matters which does not recognize the limits of reason in this field, which cannot banish fear, and which becomes lost in the category of the noncommittal. The donkey boasts that she is the leader of a girls' group that has "very interesting religious discussions." What are these discussions like? "I always say to the girls: Girls, even in faith we are supposed to use our reason. No one is intended to swallow hook, line and sinker, as the saying is." [25]

When the donkey's attention is called by Mary to her great task, the animal is plagued by curiosity. She would like to learn something to catch the attention "to carry back to our group of girls." Theological speculation and interesting disclosures cannot bring us further. Mary's request to the donkey, "For the present just do as I do and bear your master on," [26] makes everything else seem inessential by comparison with service to God.

"Perhaps some day," says Mary devoutly; everything else seems for the Christian superfluous. If in *Heaven's My Destination* war is declared on the sectarian fanatic, so in this play it is declared on the theological speculator. To this end Wilder also employs anachronism. The donkey, playing a Biblical trump card, says: ". . . as the Authorized Version has it." [27] Is this a hint that even in the earliest age of Christianity, just as in 1611, the battle over quotations had supplanted the Christianity of action and passive waiting?

Hepzibah is something like the representative of the belief in the Messiah. She says: "When the Messiah comes these things will be made clear, but until then I intend to exercise my reasoning faculty. My theory is this . . ." [28]

Again and again she begins in rabbinical manner to ratiocinate and theorize. But she is living in a time that has already brought the fulfillment. She has once already even paid her reverence to this fulfillment—Mary reminds her of this—and yet she cannot quite live in a manner in keeping with it.

The individual's excessive sense of importance, the disarrangement of the religious by the intellect—especially where the latter is small in scope, as with Hepzibah, where so-called intellectual endeavors are mingled with mere chatter—these things were such as to detract from the development of religious sentiment. No less adverse is the fear of being ridiculous, which is exemplified by Wilder in *Now the Servant's Name Was Malchus.*

In this play Wilder administered a lesson to an age extraordinary blasé in religious questions. The play's point of departure was, in altered form, the passage from the Gospel according to John, Chapter 18, Verse 10. At the very outset of the play Wilder begins to line up the perspectives: Malchus in Heaven is watching at the ordering of the "cases" of the deceased. Christ asks him which star especially is to be awarded him, and there follows the scene in which the theme is expressed that one star in particular is marked by fate and therefore in need of redemption: the earth. (Note the reference here to *The Woman of Andros.*)

Malchus in his views of significance and insignificance has already received a lesson, and so he says to Christ that the incident in which he had his ear cut off is not really so important, but adds that in Passiontide, when the passage is repeatedly noted by Bible readers, it makes him ridiculous in the eyes of men. To this Jesus replies: "But Malchus, I am ridiculous too." [29] For his religious activity and his words are, he explains, nothing but a paradox which to humans must—discreetly stated—have appeared ridiculous. He says he has declared that he is able to help men even after their death, and that now it appears that he, like everyone else, has ceased to exist. His doctrine now is at best conceived of as illusory or imaginary. Many a person (he says) has believed that he, Christ, could have been cured of his delusion by a doctor. He is faced, he says, with the alternatives of being regarded either as divine or as ridiculous. Malchus himself now has to choose between sharing in the divine or being regarded as ridiculous; he finally wants to remain with Christ. Christ is vexation, and a stumbling block to fools.

In the short play *The Angel That Troubled the Waters,* the title refers to the Biblical passage about the Pool of Bethesda, but the plot is developed by Wilder in a way other than as developed in the Bible. Jesus does not appear in the role of healer. The significant position is taken here instead by the mysterious "newcomer," a doctor by profession who has had success in healing other people, and who now comes to the healing pool himself, sick not in body but in spirit. The physically sick ones call on him to leave the place of healing since his appearance suggests health. The newcomer says that his affliction is the guilt that must be taken from him if he is to have further successes in healing: "My work grows faint. Heal me, long-expected Love." [30] But the angel explains to him that to be healed is not his destiny, for the healer himself must be sick or wounded: "Without your wound where would your power be? It is your very remorse that makes your low voice tremble into the hearts of men. The very angels themselves cannot persuade the wretched and blundering children on earth as can one human being broken in the wheels of living. In Love's service only the wounded soldiers can serve." [31]

Only the wounded are called to service. Christianity offers examples of this in Christ, Saint Paul, some of the Apostles, and later the host of martyrs. Wilder is a great adherent of this idea, which later was to find its full development in the Abbess of *The Bridge of San Luis Rey* and in Chrysis of *The Woman of Andros*. There is a connection here with Wilder's view regarding the recession of the ego. But the wounded man in *The Angel That Troubled the Waters* is at once given a task of healing: "But come with me first, an hour only, to my home. My son is lost in dark thoughts. I—I do not understand him, and only you have ever lifted his mood. Only an hour . . . my daughter, since her child has died, sits in the shadow. She will not listen to us." [32] These pleas are addressed to him by a man who has just been healed by the water, thus confirming that—even in such a man's view—the power of healing still resides in him who has been wounded.

In the larger experimental plays metaphysical and religious questions are also discussed, but it is the dramatic attempt that repeatedly stimulates Wilder. He has always resisted the tendency—present in classicism as well as romanticism—to overestimate the individual author's worth. He gives this theme an ironic treatment in the short play *Centaur.*

A performance of Ibsen's play *The Master Builder* provides beginning and end for the discussion of poetic originality and uniqueness. In that discussion Shelley declared that the idea for the Ibsen play had been taken from a poem that he had been about to write on the day of his death. Ibsen maintains that he had it from a poem which had been hovering over the Mediterranean and then came to him in the Tyrol.

The conception of poetry as an apparition is what is important here. The thoughts are directed, by way of the *universalia ante rem,* back to Plato, to whom even Shelley finally makes reference: "It is a truth that Plato would have understood that the mere language, the words of a masterpiece, are the least of its offerings. Nay, in the world we have come into now, the languages of the planet have no value; but the impulse, the idea on Comus " 'is a miracle. . . .' " [33]

Form is not unessential for Wilder, but since the guiding idea is so important for him, what he seeks is that form which affords him his most effective expression. For him the treatment of space and time is, therefore, a task that the theater must again undertake.

The problem of time Wilder explored in *The Long Christmas Dinner*, a one-act play in which he undertook to cover the span of ninety years: "Ninety years are to be traversed in this play, which represents in accelerated motion ninety Christmas dinners in the Bayard household." [34]

In accelerated motion the plot comprises the lives of four members of the family. It is done individually, and, at the same time, with that emphasis on life's basic elements—birth, sickness, marriage, old age, and death—of which there are already hints in Wilder's early works, and which unmistakably show the principal elements of his literary anthropology.

Changes in things symbolically suggest the passage of time. The two doors, one of birth and the other of death, provide the framework of the action as they do the framework of life. The theatrical factors or properties that define the story's progress are the wig and the shawl which appear as the characters grow older.

Just as there are hints of the lapse of time, so also there are hints of the action itself. The method whereby gestures suggest actions—which was so familiar a part of his later play *Our Town*—is already present here. In both plays the players eat invisible food with invisible utensils. The object of this is to abolish the realistic theater with all its required accessories, and, above all, to achieve an abstract telescoping of time.

In addition there is another element that was also to

play a decisive part in *Our Town,* the element of constant repetition. From generation to generation the conversations remain the same. Not only the ninety years constitute *The Long Christmas Dinner,* it is also the everlasting human conversation. Our life is like idle talk: "Every least twig is wrapped around with ice. You almost never see that." [35] Even opinion of the Christmas sermon is always the same ("Lovely. I cried and cried"), not to mention the constantly recurring practical counsels or the occasions for family celebrations.

This monotony has the expected effect on the audience: a sense of the enormous force of habit, and an amazement at the nothingness of which so much of life consists. The passage of time also suggests a process of flowing, and in the action almost nothing happens aside from the usual human proceedings. Thus the flowing and the standing still seem to join to form a strange paradox.

The everlasting repetition, the little segments of life, are not time. Even the ninety years are, at most, embedded in time and not time itself. Through hints one can arrive at a realization of what time is. The prevalent theater of illusion believed that the impression of time could be conveyed by representing the action in a purposely abridged and compromised form. But according to Wilder, to represent time realistically on the stage is simply impossible. One must be able to abstract from each proceeding in order to arrive at a conception of time. This cannot be conveyed to the audience through the mere fact of their looking at the play; it must be done by awakening them to reflection.

Viewed from this standpoint, even the mere hints of action that are given on the stage become effective. These, too, are an abstraction which acquires its full reality only in its effect upon the reflecting mind of the audience. There is no stage reality, but only an action commencing in a hint onstage and attaining its own reality in reflection by the audience.

The time problem is supplemented by the treatment of the spatial problem in *Pullman Car Hiawatha*. Here, as in *The Happy Journey to Trenton and Camden*, he introduces the stage manager, the figure that later, especially in Wilder's first two big plays, would seem so strange to the European public. In both plays the stage manager creates the illusion by a very few primitive means. In *Pullman Car Hiawatha* chalk lines suggest a sleeping car and its compartments, and a few words of explanation follow. Then he calls the actors onstage and the play begins. He also takes over individual roles; thus we read in the stage directions: "substituting for some woman in an upper berth" or "substituting for Upper Five." [36] With satisfaction he comments on the course of the play, and turns to make explicit contact with the public, going so far as to call attention to the characters' thought process: "Now I want you to hear them thinking." [37] That this is deliberately arranged by him is further emphasized by the fact that the "thought intermezzo" is waved offstage again. The "position"—just as it was later in *Our Town*—is established with long-winded pedantry: "Now for its position geographically, meteorologically, astronomically, theologically considered." [38] The play director gives a whistle to call back the players just as they are going onstage, and we see, already in this play, Wilder's inclination to order things in a cosmic system.

In *The Happy Journey*, the illusion-hinting role of the play director is made especially clear as the stage directions begin at once with the radical statement, "No scenery is required in this play," [39] and the stage manager, to further underscore the studied primitive quality, reads aloud from a typescript what the secondary characters have to speak.[40] In other respects, too, the posture of the stage manager is characterized in almost the same words as in *Our Town*.

In the presentation of the journey in *Pullman Car Hiawatha* there is a kind of situational division. The situation of the train as a whole is followed by the situation of each of the compartments, and these two parts are explicitly separated by the play director. The depiction of the psychological situation of the sleeping-car passengers is followed by the geographical description. This is done not in the manner that Wilder is elsewhere so fond of using, viz., giving latitude and longitude, but in a baroque manner, giving personal place-names, such as Grover's Corners. The name occurs here for the first time in Wilder's works, but in this play it is located not in New England but Ohio. Everything is recited in popular-ballad style and a foolish tone of voice and concludes with a silly popular verse.—A field is personified and its meager statements close with a rustic rule for the weather. A tramp who has been riding the rails then makes a brief appearance, and takes his leave with a quotation from Goethe which he mistakenly ascribes to Schiller. Then the town of Parkersburg, Ohio appears, with grotesque statements about the effect of alcohol, and this leads to a quartet of all four characters.

With the "weather forecast" Wilder is again moving along his old favorite ways. It is pseudo-precise realism, and one of his later interests—hours personified as philosophers—is anticipated here. Ten o'clock is identified with Plato, who sees not only the images but the reality; Epictetus' function here is to sing God's praises; and the series ends with Augustine.

Another of Wilder's favorite topics is the giving of the astronomical position, a feature to which we must now devote special attention. This datum is rendered by the persons of the actors, who represent the solar system. Their "language" is the swelling and diminishing hum directed by the stage manager. The "tone of the earth" is composed of the humming of the cities, of the workers and of the other persons, as well as the "thinking murmur" of the passengers. The idea of sorrow—which in *Servant Malchus* is so important for explaining the special nature of the earth, and is so revealing for the interpretation of a passage in *The Skin of Our Teeth*—is not mentioned.

The metaphysical note that is to be found in the "weather forecast" is supplemented in the theological note, without however the relationships being always clearly definable. The Archangels Michael and Gabriel appear—without there being a clear reference to their angelic character—as workers. Their mode of action clearly shows the beginnings of the later Wilderian considerations. They speak with two women, one of whom is dead and the other insane. They deny the dead woman a return to life. (There is no denial of this in scenes of this kind in Wilder's later plays.) The conversation with the dead woman shows the unendingly melancholy love of earth, a love that is based in part on an intense familiarity with all everyday things, but which also already contains the pacifying transition to the eternal.

The idea that the one who suffers has deeper insight is already expressed in this play, in a paradox, for the insane person, being a sufferer, is the very one that has this insight: ". . . Everyone is so childish, so absurd. They have no logic. These people are all so mad. . . . These people are like children; they have never suffered." [41]

This play much more than others, then, points ahead to Wilder's future dramatic technique and philosophy of life.

A Life in the Sun

THE FIRST publicly known version of *A Life in the Sun* was staged at the 1955 Edinburgh Festival. For this production there was, as yet, no definitive text, and even during the rehearsals Wilder constantly made alterations in the play. In Germany, in the years following the first performance, the drama was available to a small circle of readers in a hectographed edition originally meant just for stage use [under the title *Die Alkestiade*]. A definitive American edition of the text has not been published to date. In April 1960 Fischer Verlag brought out the German text as one in its series of pocket editions.[1]

Wilder was dissatisfied with his first attempt. This, and possibly another thought that was forcing itself on him (a comparison with the *Alcestis* of Euripides, from which Wilder purposely meant by the altered title to differentiate himself), led to repeated corrections and reworkings of the play. Apart from formal dramaturgic interests, the story of Alcestis occupied Wilder so intensively because it offered a special object for his attempts to interpret the pre-Christian forms of faith—especially those of classical antiquity—as precursors of Christianity.

The first mention of Alcestis in Wilder's works occurs in

The Woman of Andros, and it is a mention of the *Alcestis* of Euripides. Preparing for a symposium, Chrysis deliberates on whether she should choose the *Alcestis* for her recital from ancient works: " 'What shall I read?' she asked herself. '. . . Something from Homer? . . . No. . . . Nor would they understand the *Oedipus at Colonus.* The *Alcestis?* The *Alcestis?* " [2]

In *The Ides of March,* where much space is given to religious speculations, another ancient poetic work comes up. It is the so-called *Alcestiad* of Catullus, offered in the form of a story. The fable, told in fragmentary style, takes up the beginning of the action concerning Alcestis, as well as Alcestis' conversation with the shepherds. The story's broad commencement is in conflict with a premature and abrupt ending in which the interpretation suggested is not realized in its details.[3]

What Wilder has in mind in this passsge in *The Ides of March* is an idea which was already posed in Plato's *Symposium:* whether great poetry is the work solely of the human spirit or is inspired by the gods. One is further reminded of Plato's *Symposium* by the fact that in Wilder's play the Alcestis theme is twice mentioned in connection with a symposium, on which Plato's work says the following:

> Of this, Pelias' daughter Alcestis gives sufficient testimony for the Greeks. She alone was willing to die for her husband . . . and when she had done this she seemed glorious to all gods and humans. For though many accomplish glorious deeds, the gods have given only to a certain number the reward of releasing their souls again from Hades. They release their souls because of amazement at their deed. Thus the gods too give highest honor to care and virtue that arise out of love.[4]

The voluntary proxy death that releases a soul from the realm of the departed is the essence of the Alcestis myth.

But this does not exhaust the myth's significance for Wilder, who sees in it the means for discussing some of the questions he has already raised in his earlier works. One of these is the bridging of the gulf between man and God; another is the clarification of man's religious knowledge.

In choosing the classical tragic form for his drama of Alcestis, Wilder is in a certain way following in the tradition of Euripides, even though in his choice of title he wishes to suggest a difference between the Greek drama and his own. Wilder's title is meant to show that he is not concerned merely with the paradigmatic form of Alcestis but especially with what is happening. Apollo says in the Prologue: "I have come in order to give origin to a saga—to cause a story to begin, . . . a story that will be told many times." [5]

The work of retelling the story of Alcestis in the ancient drama form has occupied Wilder for about half a decade. Even with the deviations he allowed himself, his use of the ancient drama form was something unheard of, for he was forced by it to introduce "naturalistic" stage properties and a "naturalistic" play, things which he had largely avoided till then. The altered situation is already evident in the introductory stage notes, for here the physical objects are not replaced by suggestive aids, as in Wilder's earlier plays. But the reduction of the stage image to few elements, as provided in classical plays, spared Wilder the need of capitulating to the theater of illusion, against which he had previously warned.

Wilder divides his play into three acts, deviating from the *Alcestis* of Euripides, which consists of a Prologue and seven scenes. It is, however, highly questionable that Wilder meant his three acts to be understood as acts in the usual sense of the term. In the transition from the drama to the satyr play, Wilder's Apollo—who plays the same role as

Wilder's previous stage manager, standing at the proscenium column just as the latter did—declares: "Everything is
prepared for the postlude—the satyr play, the conclusion of
this serious trilogy, *A Life in the Sun*." [6]

Though Euripides' *Alcestis* is not a trilogy, there were
such when Greek drama was at its height. *A Life in the Sun*
is naturally not a direct imitation of them. But each of its
three acts must be accorded a greater independent weight
than is the case with the average modern three-act drama.

The play's solid structure has a kind of classic quality,
but this is not to be regarded merely as a copy, variation, or
modification of a classical design. Wilder is thoroughly
aware that to follow a classical pattern too closely could
blur the whole meaning.

The emphasis on the play's individual acts is further
increased by the fact that the action of each is divided from
the others by the span of twelve years, thus assuring the play
a kind of classic homogeneity. The choice of the number
twelve, however, is another reference to the report of an
event (though twelve is also of course the decisive number in
the classical epic) .

What we regard as the classic form of drama can also be
seen, however, in the use of a number of structural elements
proper to the classical drama itself. All three parts of the
play observe the unity of time. The Royal Palace of Pherae
serves as background, just as the royal palace often does in
Greek drama. Within the individual acts the day's time-
scheme is strictly adhered to. The beginnings of the acts are
similar in form, with the figure of the night watchman
appearing first. The Third Act of course varies from the first
two in that the old night watchman has been replaced by a
young one. He begins with the same words as his predeces-
sors in Acts One and Two, but refrains from going into
further details. Symmetry is also introduced in the First and

the Third Act with the dispute between Death and Apollo. In the middle Act this dispute is absent; at the central point of the play comes Alcestis with her great decision.

Wilder lays great stress on the observance of unity of action, avoiding subsidiary plots as far as possible. The absence of division by scenes is a further guarantee of a unified stage image. The main character's almost continuous presence on the stage reinforces the impression of the play's unity and compactness.

The plot exposition was a more difficult task for Wilder than for Euripides, who in this as in later plays adhered to the prologue pattern. The question of exposition was in any case easier for him than for Wilder, who was not so strongly bound by laws of drama as were the Greeks of the fifth century, and whose theme was not nearly so familiar to his public as was the case with the Greek public.

In Wilder's play the exposition is made primarily by three characters: Death, Apollo, and the night watchman. With Death and Apollo, the theme of the drama is at once denoted to be a metaphysical disputation, and therewith *A Life in the Sun* ceases to be in the category of realistic plays in the scholastic sense of the word. In his exposition the night watchman partly assumes the role of the stage manager in earlier plays, without the possibility of exchanging roles in the later course of the play, as did the stage manager in *Our Town*.

Unity is further assured by the entire play's being centered on the person of Alcestis. In creating his constellation of characters, Wilder has used her as the basic point of reference. The life of Alcestis is, so to speak, the intersecting point of the two worlds, the earthly and the metaphysical, the latter including also its inadequately intelligible spokesmen, Tiresias and the shepherd.

Alcestis is the play's protagonist; the antagonists are to

be found in the metaphysical sphere: Apollo and Death. Apollo is here thought of not only as a divine being and divine voice, but as a divine person whose realm is above and beneath all humans. The rest of the world of Greek deities is not of particular interest in *A Life in the Sun* and is mentioned only marginally.

But in considering the religious theme we must keep in mind how strongly the play is tied to the central character. She is the only human creature to appear again and again. The other characters either appear only in the course of the action, or—like the old watchman, Aglaia, and Admetus— they depart from the play before the action is completed.

How important Wilder considers it to keep Alcestis constantly in view is seen by comparing her with Chrysis in *The Woman of Andros*. Chrysis is dead, but life in Brynos continues to be influenced by her. In *A Life in the Sun*, Wilder could have found a similar solution, especially since ancient drama itself had such examples to offer, though not in Euripides' *Alcestis*.[7] But the mutual encounter of divine and human beings probably seemed to him to promise the greatest effect for presenting the three great phases of Alcestis' life. Alcestis meets the divine call and the divine sign: as a young woman who expects personal clarity from Apollo's sanctuary; as a wife who is ready to sacrifice her own life; and as guardian and guide for erring man led astray by his impulses.

Alcestis' greatness and her maturity are brought home to us with special force in the Second Act. In contrast to those around her, Alcestis has at once a clear perception of the message from Delphi. An almost unimaginably great offer by the god must be matched by a human sacrifice on the greatest scale. Such a sacrifice must not be conceived of as expiation but as a deed of love. In human terms the weight of Alcestis' sacrifice is very clear; she loves her children and

Admetus, she clings to life and the sun's light. She further increases this sacrifice by calling upon Admetus to take another wife after she is dead.

The greater part of Act Two of *A Life in the Sun* has roughly the same content as the corresponding part of Euripides' drama. In the latter, unlike Wilder's play, the decision is not immediately followed by the act, and there is a quite different starting situation. Euripides' Alcestis makes her sacrifice only after Admetus' parents—who in her opinion should have had to sacrifice themselves—refuse to do this. She has two further reasons: she does not want to live with her children and separated from Admetus, and she desires fame after death.

In Euripides the desire for fame after death is an important motive. Alcestis is praised by the world around her for her deed, and Pheres, who is careless of fame after death, is despised. Honor and posthumous fame, for Euripides, are also clearly apparent in the fact that Alcestis, after her great decision, continues to live with Admetus for quite some time. Euripides uses this to give his play a still greater tragic density. The audience knows that the decision of Alcestis can no longer be revoked and that for an apportioned time she and Admetus will continue in the tragic splendor of her great honor, but also in the shadow of their final parting through death.

Euripides has entwined the figure of Alcestis much more strongly with earthly life than has Wilder, in whose play she appears at once as a seeker of God and as such gives to the play's first act its central theme. Entwined with earthly things, Alcestis' expiring life and her death have, in Greek drama, a burdensome and oppressive gravity. In *A Life in the Sun,* as in the *Alcestis,* the central figure has great love for life; but in the *Alcestis* this love bears the sign of deep tragedy, for beyond this love waits the shadow realm, nothingness. "The dead are nothing." [8] "I am nothing." [9]

It can now be understood why Wilder left out the figure of old Pheres entirely. In the metaphysical conception of his drama the anxious love of life was not essential. It is also understandable that Admetus' manner as seen by Euripides had to be altered for Wilder's play. The wishes of the dying Alcestis are also correspondingly different in Euripides. She cannot award Admetus happiness in life as well as life itself after her death. She is not so selfless as to wish her husband to enter a new marriage, and she reproaches her parents for not being willing to sacrifice their aged life for her young life. It appears natural to her that young life must be preserved above all.

In the *Alcestis* of Euripides, however, there is also the divine will:

> But some god has willed it so. And so it is.
> Good, then! Repay what I have done for you.
> I do not ask you for an equal return,
> For nothing can be as precious as life.[10]

What is left at the last is only to acquiesce in the divine will. There is no prospect toward a future, since the highest value remains life.

Wilder has now made Admetus into a special figure, whose great qualities make it understandable that for such a man Alcestis is willing to die. The lack of courage, which makes Euripides' Admetus appear not especially manly, is now corrected by Wilder, though not to the extent of making his Admetus a hero.

Some qualities that distinguish the Admetus of Euripides have also been adopted by Wilder, as for example his hospitality, which earns him the love of Apollo. (In Euripides, Apollo also esteems Admetus' sense of justice.) But hospitality is not Admetus' only prominent quality;

Wilder's Admetus is characterized by a sum of good qualities that make him, so to speak, a "new human being."

At first sight Admetus is disappointing. The shepherd compares him unfavorably with Hercules. Admetus himself is thoroughly conscious of his modest attributes.

Admetus is not dependent on outward power; his power has other sources. It is based on the capacity to forgive, and, above all, on trust in the gods. His piety, submissive to their will, is in the state of grace. He can renounce kingly status and retire in favor of liberty.

The tone of *A Life in the Sun* is softened by there being no mention of the proxy death which is asked of Admetus' parents and by which they could have saved their son. The elimination of Pheres means, moreover, that there is no parallel to Scene Four of Euripides' play, where there is a terrible argument between father and son during Alcestis' funeral procession.

But there is something further to be said about the figure of Pheres and the above scene—something quite important for Wilder perhaps, for it involves the discussion of custom and law.[11] In the tragedy of Euripides, Pheres appears at the funeral in order to adorn his daughter-in-law at the *prothesis,* and to express his sympathy to his son. He carries out that which custom requires, for, he believes, it is custom that endures.

When Pheres appears, Admetus breaks out into insulting and infuriating words. Pheres replies that custom and law by no means require fathers to die in place of their sons: [12]

PHERES: I begot you and brought you up as my heir,
  But I am not bound to die for you.
  There has never been a tradition in Greece
  That fathers must die for their sons.
  Your fate, whether sad or fortunate,
  Is your fate. What I owed you, you have.

> Many subjects, wide possessions, will you inherit
> From me, as I did from my father.
> Have I curtailed your property or rights?
> Don't die for me, and I'll not die for you! [13]

Pheres' thoughts remain in the realm of the νόμος. Their meaning becomes clear when they are compared with the dispute between Apollo and Death at the beginning of the drama. Apollo appears armed in the palace of Pheres, in order to win that which has fallen to him:

APOLLO: Be not afraid: I want what is right and reasonable.

DEATH: If you want only what is right, then why the bow and arrows?

APOLLO: I am accustomed always to carry them.

DEATH: And to help that family more than is right.

APOLLO: He is my friend. His sorrow oppresses me.

DEATH: So do you want to rob me of the second soul too?

APOLLO: I did not rob you of her husband's soul.

DEATH: Then why is he above ground, not below? [14]

Death is afraid that a breach might be made in the old "law." The rest of the dispute between Apollo and Death concerns first of all Apollo's argument that it cannot hurt Death to wait. Death is unwilling to accept this argument, maintaining that "right" is on his side:

APOLLO: So you will not fulfill my wish?

DEATH: No. You know me too well to need to ask.

APOLLO: You are hated by mortals and by gods alike.

DEATH: You cannot have your way in everything.[15]

Death knows that by law everything is subject to him. He is not willing to suspend this law nor even to restrict its effects. But Apollo means to break through the barriers, and his instrument for this is Hercules.

All those who swear by the "law of tradition"— including Pheres—are, then, in league with Death. But Apollo, using Hercules, ushers in the new epoch; he creates the "change." Wilder's ideas—which we have still to consider in detail—must have been especially responsive to this process, bringing as it does the great "turning point" for natural man.

Euripides' words, to be sure, hint rather than fully substantiate. Alcestis, who has become the object of the disputes of the metaphysical power, acquiesces to the divine will but only dimly feels and only by necessity affirms her fate.

She does not evolve anything like a new theology. With her person, it is true, a new mythic process is introduced. Until her deed of sacrifice, Orpheus and Eurydice were the mythic figures with whom were linked the ides of breaching the barrier of death. Admetus himself—in Wilder's version —does fail, in his will to win back Alcestis, because he has not been given the power of song. But now Alcestis, with the god and the hero, opens the new way. The assault on death, on its seemingly eternal law, is consummated by the proxy sacrifice. Death is conquered by death.

In discussing the structure of the beginning of *A Life in the Sun,* we pointed out that the antagonist is to be found in the moral realm. Agis, who might still be considered among the human characters, is eliminated from consideration because his effect in *A Life in the Sun* is too small. He appears for the first time in the Third Act, in the role of villain who has murdered Admetus, seized power and made

Alcestis a slave. These horrible deeds we see only in their results, for they must have taken place in the twelve years that intervene between the Second and the Third Acts. But finally Agis is too small in his capacity to be considered as the antagonist. In the Third Act of his play Wilder shows him in the midst of a plague, and the king's fear and wild screaming reveal his utter weakness.

The appearance of Hercules, in the *Alcestis* and in *A Life in the Sun,* is motivated with his coming to the Court of Pherae as guest. At first there does not seem to be much difference between the two versions, and yet there are nuances even at the outset which allow us to draw differing inferences for the further course of the two plots. Wilder's Hercules—who in his outward behavior is a rowdy and wencher—appears at the palace of Admetus and Alcestis to "ask a single question." [16] In Euripides, he stops for lodging on his way to Thrace.

The difficulty in shaping the character of Hercules lay in his dual nature, for greater prominence would of necessity have to be given either to his human or his divine qualities. This prompted Wilder to make Hercules more human, with occasional doubts and afflictions. Hercules expects Alcestis to answer the question as to whether he is really a demigod. It remains unanswered, for Alcestis dies at the moment when she is to give him her answer.

In Euripides, the personal nature of Hercules is not discussed. His deeds appear as great and difficult achievements, which because of his abilities can be required of him. Here Euripides does not give much direct presentation. Thus the fight with Death is a planned attack from ambush. Wilder, who was not without an instinct of his own for such effects, started to portray a Hercules conscious of his own limitation, but had to abandon the idea of creating such an effect. *A Life in the Sun* offers no glimpses into the struggles in the lower regions; one sees, at the last, only Alcestis after she has been led back to earth by Hercules.

In the *Alcestis*, Hercules is helpful, friendly, and always rather coarse, which offers Euripides an occasion for presenting situations that seem grotesque. He stops his ears against hearing the speech of Admetus, and his noisy reveling at the Court of Pherae anger those present, for he knows that the palace is in mourning, even if he does not know that it is for Alcestis.

Euripides has not brought Hercules into the psychic complications that Wilder has. His fundamental interest is the question that he puts to Alcestis, and he hopes that she, the one who knows many things, can answer it. Nor is Euripides' Hercules burdened with a "past,"—his past attempt to violate Alcestis—and in his manner he is not inhibited by excessive reverence.

Euripides' Hercules is only a transient guest, and the ancient quality that he puts to the test is the quite simple one of hospitality. By this quality Admetus has won the favor of Apollo, and his behavior toward the coarse and noisy fellow who now appears is to that deity proof of how highly he esteems the virtue of hospitality. Also the task that Hercules then has to fulfill is easily understood: He is the helper of humans and is therefore supposed to bring back the dead woman.

In the sphere of the gods, the decisive figure is Apollo. We have seen that in Euripides too he is involved in the opening scene in a dialogue with Death. From the introduction in Euripides' play we learn more than from Wilder about the story's mythological prehistory. Apollo had had to serve anonymously as a slave at the court of Admetus for one year, because he had killed the Cyclops, who had forged for Zeus the lightning bolt with which the Father of the Gods had killed Apollo's son Asclepius.

This account in Euripides reveals a certain gratitude of Apollo toward Admetus for the latter's good treatment of him, and also contains an acknowledgement of Admetus' piety. Wilder does not mention the story at all. Wilder's play does not begin with the great introductory explanatory monologue of Apollo, but proceeds directly to the disputation between Apollo and Death, the fundamental powers of light and of darkness.

Apollo characterizes the sphere of Death: "Death, you live in the dark." [17] The god himself stands for light. His appearance is identified with light. The introductory stage directions indicate the newly rising day and also the new influence of Apollo: "Shimmer of dawn—gradually the light rises to full radiance—during the entire scene Apollo looks into the distance toward the rising sun—cool, poised, with a slight smile on his lips." Death then asks Apollo in which of his capacities he has come, as healer of the sick, consequently in connection with Asclepius (there was already a reference to this in the circumstances of *The Woman of Andros*), or as singer. Here, then, is a direct allusion to Apollo as "bringer of light and spreader of life." This duality of Apollo and Death, Light and Darkness moves through the entire play. When the watchman begins with the call, "It is dawn, it is dawn," [18] the words tell us more than simply the time of day. They tell us that the time of Apollo's dominion, the time of light, is now beginning.

The concentration on the figure of Apollo in the world of Greek myth—the rest of the world of the gods receives at most a mere mention—allows the metaphysical problem of triumph over death to emerge with special prominence in union with the symbolism of light. Wilder, more than Euripides, has freed Apollo from intrinsic human traits. Although he is the god of light, Apollo is discernible by men only to a very limited degree. He is seen only by Death and by none of the other characters in the play. The production notes for the play indicate two possible ways for Apollo to make his appearances. On the one hand, he appears on the roof of the palace clad in a golden garment and surrounded by a strong light; in this aspect he is not discernible at all to the human world around him. Otherwise he makes his appearances through the palace door or the gate of the court, clad in a dark blue cloak and hood, and only occasionally a ray of light makes his garment gleam: a hint that Apollo—i.e., divinity—cannot be directly discerned by men.[19]

The visible revelation of God would be the final solution of the problem of cognition, but it does not occur. Thus Death can ask, with open mockery, "Have you come today to show us some great sign or wonder?" [20] To this direct opening question there is no direct answer in the ensuing dialogue. Instead the question is interrupted by the involved and rather noisy entrance of the night watchman and his brief explanation of the time, place and action. Death insistently repeats his question, trying to learn whether Apollo will allow Admetus or Alcestis to descend to the lower regions, and Apollo gives no answer. If men are denied direct knowledge of God, and if the deity does not even give Death any direct information concerning its signs and wonders, then life's meaning is hidden from mankind. Is the search for it in vain?

In the Prologue, Apollo tells Death: "I have come in order to give origin to a legend—to cause a story to begin —a story that will be told many times." [21] The deity wills the institution of a story, and needs man to attain its end. God's purpose is not clear to man, for man is too engrossed in anthropomorphic ideas. Old Aglaia reverts to this in her words to Alcestis: "What do you believe they are, Princess? You are not imagining them as *humans*?" [22]

The unknowable deity gives the human world order and meaning. It is not a forever static meaning, but one of purposeful development and change: a story shall begin, an example shall be shown. The deity is in the world but not of the world, so that man is constantly in search of it. Man's endeavor cannot be in vain, for the divine plan guarantees that this endeavor has meaning.

Man perceives the deity only in hints or riddles. How can he come nearer to it? Can he bridge this gulf that Wilder again shows us in this latest work? Is there any kind of certainty of faith? Wilder devotes the very first act of his drama to this question. The dramatic action, which in Euripides fills the frame of the entire play, is relegated by Wilder to the Second Act.

In the First Act, Alcestis wishes to go to Delphi to visit the god's abode and there obtain full clarity. The phases of human life, on which the division of the entire play is based, become visible here in another than the biological sense, because the question, What clearness is meant here? has its context in the springtime of human history. The topic of "clarity" is introduced at this stage by a remark of the old woman servant Aglaia that Alcestis should remember how she won Admetus: the apparition of Apollo had guided her and brought her into a critical situation. To this Alcestis replies brusquely, "We have heard enough of such feverish dreams, such hallucinations, Aglaia. It is time we demanded certainty. The open, unconcealed presence of the god—this is to be found at Delphi." [23]

Aglaia retorts to this juvenile demand for knowledge: "Open? Unconcealed? Even the priestess at Delphi speaks as in a delirium. Who has ever heard of the gods' letting themselves be seen clearly and distinctly?" [24]

The figure of Tiresias, which appears in the *Phoenissae* and the *Bacchae* of Euripides but not in his *Alcestis,* is introduced by Wilder into his play immediately following these words of Aglaia, quite differently from the way tradition has him appear. Like Hercules, Tiresias is an instrument of the god—not by his physical power but by his words.

But his words are hard to understand, and, it appears, hardly intelligible either, for he seems to have no clear idea of the message he is supposed to deliver. The blind man's violent temper prevents him at times from speaking calmly and collectedly. So forgetful and incoherent is he that a boy who accompanies him has to remind him of what he wants to say.

Even one of the shepherds is astonished at Tiresias' language and behavior, and criticizes the gods for choosing such a person as their instrument: "That was Tiresias? That doddering old man? Can't they find any better messenger than that? Can't they say what they have to say more distinctly?" [25]

Tiresias, then—improbably enough—is supposed to be the messenger of the gods. The god Apollo is supposed to have assumed the form of one of the shepherds, although at first sight they all seem quite ordinary herdsmen. What is conspicuous about them, however, is that each of them embodies one particular characteristic of Apollo. Such an embodiment, moreover, may occur in others too, such as the pious Admetus:

"If Tiresias is right, Apollo is here in Thessaly. But maybe the forgetful old man's instructions were to tell us that Apollo is here, but divided among many persons—among us four shepherds, and others too! For example, how do things stand with King Admetus?" [26]

The idea that the deity finds an embodiment in a person possessing a characteristic of the deity had already been a theme of *The Cabala*. In that story the idea interested Wilder primarily in connection with the theories regarding myths. His consideration at that time was focused mainly on the efficacy of the deity; now—as in almost all of Wilder's other works—the main topic of discussion is the possibility of man's attaining to knowledge through faith.

The gods can supply the meaning of that which man is unable to comprehend. A too-strong desire for direct knowledge of God is a barrier to recognition of the divinely meaningful signs in this world. Alcestis must first renounce her wish for direct knowledge before she can share in the consciousness of the worlds of the gods.

At first, in a conversation with one of the shepherds, Alcestis feels depressed in status almost to the level of the animals by her incomprehension of the divine:

ALCESTIS: But if we do not understand, then our life is hardly better than that of the animals.

SHEPHERD: No, Mistress, to understand means to see something whole. But do we humans ever see a thing whole, and how it ends? . . . a part of something larger than we are able to see.[27]

Admetus of course has had faith in being part of something larger that was ordained by the gods. His love for Alcestis seemed to him a guarantee that the rule of the deity had meaning. But now the seeming absurdities come upon him, and possibly they can shake his owner inner security: Alcestis wants to go to Delphi, and only at the close of the First Act does she finally consent to marry Admetus. Again the god is in league with Admetus: like Admetus, Apollo too extends his hands toward Alcestis. The gestures of the man and of the god become one. This applies to the version of the play which shows Apollo among human beings. However the manner whereby the god imparts significance by a gesture is not visible to Admetus, but only to the audience.

The worst trial of Admetus' faith comes in the Second Act. If the shepherds' behavior had at times been very questionable and even words of doubt and criticism of the god had come from the mouth of one of them, at the same time many hints were to be heard, such as the statement of Tiresias that Apollo would be concealed in one of the shepherds. But now the shepherd is the very one who delivers the mortal wound to Admetus.

Admetus of course never goes beyond being a questioner to become a doubter, as Alcestis does. Alcestis, after the behavior of Tiresias seems to have shown that even the god at his seat at Delphi is not going to give religious security and clarity, expresses her doubt very forcefully: "Some say that you [Apollo] do not exist at all. . . . Are we humans to be left to ourselves without a sign or a word of explanation? Have we been abandoned?" [28]

These words recall a passage in Wilder's first great work, *The Bridge of San Luis Rey*: "Some say that we shall never know, and that to the Gods we are like the flies that the boys kill on a summer day, and some say, on the contrary, that the very sparrows do not lose a feather that has not been brushed away by the finger of God." [29]

A Life in the Sun does not stop, however, at describing man's place in relation to God. In it a sign is demanded and a road is sought: "Then we must find our way alone . . . . And life is a foolish groping and grasping at this and that . . . a senseless thing, full of passions . . . ." [30]

Alcestis asks in despair, yet she goes her way. By her the decision is made in the Second Act: she elects to die in place of her husband. This deed is within the meaning of the opening disputation between Apollo and Death. By this deed she has changed the world.

Apollo had once already spoken—apart from the question of Alcestis' personal fate—about the beginning of the "change" in the human race: "Human beings have begun to understand me. At first they were like animals—and yet not like animals—no, wilder, more easily frightened. Like caught animals—themselves their own cage. Then they became conscious of two things, and they lifted their heads. One was my Father's thunder, which raised their fear to reverence. The other was my sunlight, for which they wished to thank me. In trying to do this they discovered language, and I gave them the gift of song. Those were signs, and they knew them." [31]

Apollo here makes the "change" apply to the entire human race. This "change" has brought man from the purely animal state to the possession of the gift of song. One of Apollo's characteristics has thereby been realized.

Apollo has now come forth in order to institute one of the great stories of humanity, a story that also contains a human change. This time, however, it is not a development that is involved, but a struggle with an unyielding power, Death.

But instituting the story requires the god's withdrawal into the background in the Second Act. Alcestis must die her proxy death entirely of her own volition. She is thereby in a position to breach the wall, threatening and seemingly firm, that has been raised around the fate of the human race.

The essence of death, which conditions the nature of man, is explained in an earlier conversation between Alcestis and the shepherd. The latter is speaking of the two kinds of death: "For I have always noticed that there are two kinds of death: one that is an end, and one that is an advance, pregnant with that which follows. . . . Let me die this latter death . . . —for it would preserve me from the other, which I dread: just ceasing to exist—becoming mere dust in a grave." [32]

Human mortality remains a fact after the death of Alcestis, but Death has lost its absolute and unconditional dominion. With this deed, Alcestis meets the deity halfway, for she offers her life of her own free will, in order to preserve that life forever.

The fact of suffering in the world seems to contradict the idea that the gods are loving toward men. Death, the great adversary of life, makes an ironic allusion to this in his opening conversation with Apollo: "When the gods draw near to men, sooner or later someone is killed. Am *I* able today to greet an honored guest in *my* kingdom?" [33]

In this connection the ancients' notion that a god has a special locality is significant. Death returns to this subject:

DEATH: Apollo *loves* Thessaly. Apollo *loves* the Royal House of Pherae! Go back to Mount Olympus where you belong! This whole idea of love—it's hard to say whom it makes unhappier, yourself or these wretched creatures. Whenever you attempt to enter their lives, you are like a giant in a small room: with every movement you smash something.—And whom will you torment today? The King? Or his bride?

APOLLO: You.

DEATH: Me? Me? So you've decided to love me too? No, thank you! [34]

Deity and its nearness mean danger for human beings. To Tiresias, perception of this truth has become second nature; amid all his confusion he holds fast to it as to a kind of elementary knowledge that even the pious Admetus obviously lacks:

TIRESIAS: . . . A great honor and a great danger has fallen to Thessaly's lot.

ADMETUS: A danger, Tiresias?

TIRESIAS: An honor and a danger. . . . Don't you here in Thessaly know even the simplest and most self-evident things? [35]

The mortal injury at the hands of the shepherd, which to human reason must have seemed completely senseless, can now be seen to lie in the nature of godhood. Suffering and hurt are also part of the divine plan—and therefore part of the divine love.

But Tiresias knows only of the danger. His knowledge of the love of the gods for men is not extensive. Almost like Death he complains, and he accuses too. The brief scene in which Admetus makes a further inquiry is revealing:

ADMETUS: . . . You said something about a *danger,* Tiresias?

TIRESIAS: (*already half through the doorway*) : Danger! Obviously, you simpleton. When *they* (*abrupt gesture heavenwards*) approach, it's always dangerous.

ADMETUS: But my father said that Apollo always loved Thessaly. . . .

TIRESIAS: Yes—loved, loved, loved! Those up there should keep their love to themselves! Look at *me:* five hundred, six hundred years old, and so much loved by the gods that I am not permitted to die. If the gods would not love men, we would all be happy.[36]

Tiresias here is not an atheist. He believes in the gods' existence; he is their mouthpiece. The relationship of gods to men and men to gods is something he cannot view in the normal terms of human feeling and reason. To him, it would be best for humanity's happiness if *amor dei,* in every sense of the term, would leave the world altogether.

The deficiency of the deity's love, and—again according to Tiresias—the seeming advisability of a distant attitude toward the deity, show the gulf that exists between man and the deity. This question is taken up once more in the speech of a shepherd, who gives his opinion on the question of bridging the gulf:

"Maybe there is another way—a way to cross over the gulf. I mean—maybe they know a way to go and bring up people they love—bring them up closer to themselves, I mean. . . . It has slowly dawned on me that King Admetus has something that none of these other heroes have . . . What would life be good for, Princess, unless now and then a new *kind* of men came into the world—and a new kind of women?" [37]

At this place in the text Wilder's stage notes give a strong hint: Admetus appears in a cloak similar to Apollo's, or Apollo and Admetus appear. "And would that not perhaps be the way that these who love unhappily (he points upward) would try to throw a bridge across the gulf?" [38]

Concerning "the new kind of men and women," Wilder had already asked questions in his early works. Now for the first time, however, he portrays in this connection, and in full detail, the idea of a proxy death. This transforms Alcestis, and from her the treatment of the motif, "Return to Life," gains another aspect. Up to now Wilder had treated this theme almost as an attempt: Man after death longed to return to his earthly home. His pleas were finally granted, but repelled and disappointed by the unconcern, banality, and lovelessness of human life, he returns again to his final domain.

After her return to the world, Alcestis at first remains there, but not in a state of earthly happiness, for her fortune has greatly changed: she has become a slave. Her position in relation to the deity has become different, and it is this change that gives the entire Third Act of *A Life in the Sun* its special meaning. Alcestis lives no longer in uncertainty, she no longer complains of the deity's concealment and the inadequacy and uncertainty of human knowing.

In this context, Wilder now makes a new approach to the problem of theodicy, which still torments Alcestis' milieu. The problem becomes visible at the beginning of the final Act, in the conversation between Epimenides and Cheriander. As the conversation shows, the theodicy question is often posed wrongly because a relationship is drawn between a negative personal experience—cruelty, murder, injustice—and the personal life of man. Such an attitude must lead in religious life to distortions and negations, and in human emotional life to revenge and retribution.

Because these oppressively negative phenomena traverse the entire world, they must, so Cheriander thinks, be ordained by the gods. Man does not have any clear insight into the entirety of such a system of things; all that is left him is to trust and hope in the wisdom of the gods. But Alcestis, from her experience and her affirmation of her chosen road, has come to declare that even a portion of life has meaning.

The theme she sounded in the First Act—"there is only one misery, and that is uncertainty"—she now takes up again in view of the despair and great misery surrounding her. After her experience of her chosen road she says to Cheriander, who is especially receptive to her words:

> "Not to know what meaning our life has. *That* is misery and despair. Great happiness once fell to my lot. Shall I now forget that? And forget *him* who gave it to me? All that has happened since came from the same hand, is part of a whole that I simply am unable to see." [39]

Alcestis can see the part only as a part. She does not confuse it with the whole. The part belongs to the whole, but is not *ipso facto* identifiable with it. If the part is taken without conceivable relation to an (unknown) whole, and taken as a temporal sequence of antithetical and mutually contradictory proceedings, such as happiness and unhappiness or of conflicting emotions such as love and hate, it can cause faith in the deity to become absurd. This has bearing on the events of the Third Act and on their evaluation by Alcestis' milieu.

But the deity recalls itself to man's memory, and makes itself understandable to him by employing extreme means, such as death. In its saving yoke, divine love and great severity are coupled together. One may say that death is a final means which God uses in order to open man's locked understanding and fix a lasting impression on man's memory. Apollo says: "Yes, I must bring destruction and devastation, for only thus will men remember my story. In all stories that remain in their memory, death plays a great role." [40]

Alcestis at the last realizes all this. For her, Apollo remains ever the god of Thessaly. But even she, at the end of her life, shortly before she is transported, cannot give an answer to the question concerning the sign. After her great experience, she no longer even asks the question. It is raised by Cheriander, who would see the sign in Alcestis herself. This she expressly denies. She is "the first of a great number who are unwilling to have this end"—i.e., do not want their final resting place to be the grave. [41] She has broken the imprisoning ring that had been placed around humanity— but she is still human. Weary, and guided by Apollo, she asks after all for her grave and her resting place.

Alcestis also achieves for the future an effect on another person. Agis, the barbarian, does not bring with him those prerequisites for knowledge of theological questions that the original inhabitants of the land of Apollo had. To him Alcestis seems a kind of witch whose return from the dead is to blame for the plague, or a sorceress who can show him the earthly road by which he could get his daughter Laodamia back from the lower regions. Alcestis can reassure Agis, without fully convincing him, by explaining that the plague is a sign not of the god's hate but of his love. With this, too, a new phase of human history has begun. From now on, the riddle of the seeming inscrutability of divine ways will agitate behind the low forehead of the barbarian.

Out of a tragedy of classical antiquity in which the compulsive force of fate (*moira*) is broken through once but not annulled in its ultimate, metaphysical effect by a proxy death, Wilder has made a drama of martyrdom. Pain, agony, and farewell are the tormenting experiences by which a surer knowledge is attained, a knowledge that includes the possibility of bridging the gulf between God and man.

In *A Life in the Sun*, the "change" of man is commensurate with the deed done in behalf of humanity. The "new man" is nearer to God, and the form of his service is clothed in humility: Alcestis is the "maidservant of maidservants," and the deity conceals itself in the lowly form of the shepherds.

⊰ 10 ⊱

The Eighth Day

In 1967, twelve years after the opening performance of *A Life in the Sun*, appeared Wilder's latest novel, *The Eighth Day*. According to all accounts, Wilder had worked a relatively long time on it. Wilder largely avoided public honors on his sixty-fifth birthday, and by that date had probably already begun the preparation of his new book.

The new novel has once again an American theme; thus it is closer in its content to *Heaven's My Destination* than to *The Ides of March* or *The Cabala* or *The Woman of Andros*. It is not so far, in externals, from *The Bridge of San Luis Rey*, inasmuch as Chapter Two is set in South America.

Whereas in *Heaven's My Destination* the shaping of the fable recalls in a way Bunyan's *Pilgrim's Progress*, in *The Eighth Day* the structural points of contact with other works of literature are not so obvious, though there is a suggestion in the fact that the time of the story is contemporaneous with the appearance of the so-called "muckraking" literature. The expression "muckraking" was first taken from that figure in *Pilgrim's Progress* who was so busy sweeping up earth's refuse that he did not see heaven's salvation. "Muckraking" as a term underwent a remarkable transformation.

Originally applied in a derogatory sense to men of letters who were fond of "stirring up filth," it then became a term of recognition for those writers who did not shrink from writing of even the worst social abuses, thus showing their desire for social change.

There is no more in Wilder's new novel to interest sociologists and politicians than there was in *Heaven's My Destination,* for the time of the story is set back from the present, essentially spanning the years 1880 to 1905. Wilder thus might have used the opportunity to depict various contemporary social problems, such as the great economic crisis of 1893–1894, and the conditions of economic monopoly that led to the anti-trust legislation of 1890.

But references to the social nadir of those years are not entirely absent from Wilder's novel, as is evidenced by his portrayal of the questionable judicial process in the story, also the tuberculosis which was still ravaging society, and the poorhouse question. But all such events of social history gain their real interest only as the characters react to them, and very often they appear, in relation to fundamental human affairs, only insofar as they are part of the whole human cosmos. For Wilder, too, they are of course an annoyance, but they do not become for him an angry obsession that blocks his vision of what he considers most important.

The novel's title at first appears enigmatic, and in the so-called "Prologue" even provocative, yet the Prologue also already gives the explanation of the title. For a writer who stands as close as Wilder does to religious tradition, the number seven has significance as the number of the Biblical days of creation including the Lord's day of rest. At the same time, Wilder is probably not unaware that the number seven was genetically a fixed element of the tradition of the Semitic peoples, and that also in later times this number was the departure point for sometimes colorful and bizarre speculations.

In the idea of progress, which governs much human thinking—American especially lies also the origin of the novel's title. In six days the world has been created, the seventh day has been the day of rest, and now—on the occasion of a New Year's address at the turn of the twentieth century—the physician Dr. Gillies announces that the eighth day, in which the process of creation is to be continued, has now begun. The whole thing assumes at once a slightly ironic tone, for the reader learns that Dr. Gillies does not much believe in what he is saying, but readily tells those who are captivated by the idea of earthly progress what they expect to hear.

Wilder shows the absurdity of narrow-minded persons by having the banker and his wife rise indignantly during Dr. Gillies' address and say, "evolution, godless evolution." These are the people who have taken the mischievous element of these reflections all too seriously. That there is some mischievousness in what he is up to Wilder leaves the reader in no doubt. He explains that Dr. Gillies addresses his words especially to the young people present, who pursue the illusion of man's further development and who still are borne along by hope, a hope that will serve as a buffer against the despair that is to come. With a wink of the eye he offers the maxim, "It is the duty of old men to lie to the young." [1]

Wilder is not working with the evolution schema, but—again—with his idea of "creative mind," which finds its expression repeatedly in all times and on all social levels in outstanding examples of the *genus humanum,* and of which ultimately all individuals may partake.

Nothing is more interesting than the inquiry as to how creativity operates in anyone, in everyone: mind, propelled by passion, imposing itself, building and unbuilding; mind—the latest-appearing manifestation of life—expressing itself in statesman and criminal, in poet and banker, in street cleaner and housewife, in father and mother—establishing order or spreading havoc; mind—condensing its energy in groups and nations, rising to an incandescence and then ebbing away exhausted; mind—enslaving and massacring or diffusing justice and beauty:

Pallas Athena's Athens, like a lighthouse on a hill, sending forth beams that still illuminate men in council;

Palestine, for a thousand years, like a geyser in the sand, producing genius after genius, and soon there will be no one on earth who has not been affected by them.[2]

Here of course Wilder, through the narrator, sounds an optimistic note, which however differs from the optimism of evolutionism: Pallas Athena becomes, like the doctrines of Palestine, the common property of all. Here, then, are possibilities for man's orientation, but owing to human weakness and imperfection, life in practice is spiteful and does not permit these possibilities to come to full maturity.

But the Prologue offers more than a kind of humorous ideological introduction. It also offers a hint of the fable itself, namely, the murder of Lansing in the American mining community of Coaltown, and the public's certain assumption that the deed was done by Ashley. We are then told the story of Ashley's mysterious liberation, and in Chapter One which follows we learn more details about the Ashley family and—in less detail—the Lansing family, both of whom are entangled in the tragedy.

A strange beginning, calculated to amaze the reader— but a beginning that wins the reader by its humor, irony, and self-irony. The further development of the story seems to show at least two types of novel: the family novel and the criminal—or better—the mystery novel. The family novel had still celebrated great triumphs as late as the 1920's, but by now had long since been declared dead. That it could now be revived in its old form is hardly conceivable, for authors lack the necessary energy and readers the necessary patience. But in Thomas Wolfe the family novel had already undergone great changes, so that it could not be called an epic family novel in the old sense of the term. Thus it was not altogether impossible for a writer to try his hand again in this genre if he employed modern structural and stylistic methods.

In his earlier novels Wilder had already displayed great experience in these methods. The structural qualities that had already been successfully used in *The Ides of March* were used again in this new novel.

The new book contains besides the Prologue six chapters, of which two[3] begin in 1902 and end in 1905. Their time spans coincide because they both relate the story of Ashley, the father in Chile, and two of his children in Chicago within this period. The first chapter spans the years 1885–1905. The fourth spans just the year 1883; it is a sample year chosen at random, but here—as sometimes elsewhere in the book—events are told which lie far beyond the chapter's time limits. In this as in other novels Wilder uses the technique of narrating certain events in the present and then either reflecting on them retrospectively from the vantage point of a later date or hinting at what the effects of those events will be. The initial and terminal dates mark focal points of the narrative, but what happens in between is arranged within a broad timespan that at times extends from earliest prehistoric ages to a time beyond the present.

The fifth chapter spans the years 1880–1905, the sixth only the Christmas season of 1905. In comparison with the time scheme of *The Ides of March*—which is, as we have seen, more comprehensive, and in which each chapter goes over previous ground and, excepting the final Book, gives only a few days' or weeks' new material—the successive chapters of *The Eighth Day* give a great deal about the entire history of the Ashley and Lansing families.

The individual chapters center on the life histories of particular persons or groups of persons. The first chapter tells of the rehabilitation and the life of the Ashley family, who have bought The Elms, the Coaltown residence that, after the father's conviction and flight, had been turned into a boarding house. This offers Wilder the opportunity to portray the fate and the struggle for existence of a conventionally declassé bourgeois family. At the same time, however, it offers him the opportunity—of which he had already made use in *Heaven's My Destination*—to portray some marginal characters and in them as in the others develop a piece of his philosophy of life.

In the second chapter the course of the fugitive Ashley's life is traced in retrospect. The mystery story now receives some illumination, for which the reader is in part prepared.

The mystery-story character of the book had in any case been somewhat muted by Wilder from the beginning. The book begins with these words:

> In the early summer of 1902 John Barrington Ashley of Coaltown, a small mining center in southern Illinois, was tried for the murder of Breckenridge Lansing, also of Coaltown. He was found guilty and sentenced to death. Five days later, at one in the morning of Tuesday, July 22, he escaped from his guards on the train that was carrying him to his execution.[4]

This reads like a police report. But the following chapter already brings the reassurance that "about five years later, the State's Attorney's office in Springfield announced that fresh evidence had been uncovered fully establishing Ashley's innocence." [5]

This second chapter affords the opportunity to enlarge upon Ashley's manner and his attitude to life. As a young man he had lost his Christian faith, and had also learned that "to submit to the will of God" meant "some last numbing demand on human fortitude." [6] But Wilder makes the very good observation that Ashley's newly gained atheistic position only delivered him to a "more abject superstition." [7] But the real basis of his development is faith, and with this we are reminded of Wilder's favorite epistle of St. Paul, a recollection that is confirmed in those important passages of the novel where hope and love are also brought into play. The author demurs and expressly directs the reader to his own treatment of this theme: "In this history there has been some discussion of hope and faith. It is too early to treat of love." [8]

We should of course not expect in this novel too explicit and crude professions of Christianity. Where we see this feature most clearly is in a story that is built into the novel. The story takes place in a prison, where the inmates have lost the consciousness of time-reckoning by the calendar, and have recovered this ability to reckon time from one of the inmates who in place of the worldly calendar gave them a church calendar, "that other calendar that strengthens our steps and confirms our joy." [9] Wilder, however, says somewhat reservedly that "religions are merely the garments of faith." [10] He does not attach himself firmly to a religion, but he does make it plain that man's constitutive qualities may find in religions their forms of expression. In the structure of the story this theme is seen, for example, in the fact that Ashley helps to build a church in Coaltown for a sect to which he does not even belong, and in Chile a church for the Catholics.

The men and women of faith are, by Wilder's characterization, invisible, only occasionally emerging into view, as at those places where their active religious life manifests itself.

Faith can found schools, but is not dependent on them. Wilder sums up the characteristics of faith: it is "fearless, not self-referent, uninteresting, humorless, so often unlearned." [11]

Those who believe are committed to the active life, although for many the results of their work are not perceptible.

Another significant characteristic of those who believe —and here is seen Wilder's basically undogmatic attitude— is that they do not stand in the cross fire of history. "No historic demands were laid upon him." [12] Thus John Ashley is to be regarded only as a link in a chain, "a stitch in a tapestry, a planter of trees, a breaker of stones on an old road to a not yet clearly marked destination." [13]

Ashley is not marked by any kind of contemporary significance, nor does he prove to be a "mature man"; on the other hand, he is distinguished by a natural sureness.

Again Wilder takes the opportunity to give further characteristics of the "man of faith," which bring him close to the "man of genius." Although the men of faith do not live consciously, they have a link to "relationships, recurrences, patterns, and laws." [14] To them clarity and far vision are granted, whereas those who consciously demand clarity show a dry and narrow spirit.

Thus Ashley can achieve rapport with his new environment, as it is given in prototype by literary tradition: he, the "family man," is the father buffeted by fate, an Odysseus, an Enoch Arden.[15]

The necessity of Ashley's orienting himself as an "outcast" in a strange world leads Wilder in turn to employ his old "identification" schema, in which the "recurrent types" appear. At first the family man is reminded, by gestures and the like, of the members of his family, but then the author commences the identification with the gods of antiquity.

Wilder brings into this book an element from still another type of novel: the novel of education, the *Bildungsroman*. This new strand is of course not heavy with great knowledge; indeed, there are places in the third chapter, telling of Roger and Lily Ashley's development, where the narrative sounds like a "success story" as Roger becomes a great journalist and Lily a celebrated singer. This has, however, at least a structural justification, since once they are successful, they discard their pseudonyms and reassume the name of their father, the fugitive whose picture still hangs on the wall of every police station.

In a brief episode in Chapter Three, John Ashley meets two didactic scholars in Chile. Both savants come from countries identified with learning: one is from Scotland, the other from Germany. Dr. MacKenzie pursues studies in comparative religion and sees two great historical developments: the deification of man, as was customary with the Egyptians, and the embodiment of Greek deities in individuals and professional classes of the present day,[16] an idea with which readers of *The Cabala* will not be unfamiliar. This doctrine of MacKenzie's does not find much of an echo with Ashley, for MacKenzie makes the reflection with much too much irony for it to appeal to the humorless Ashley. MacKenzie characterizes Ashley as a Hebrew whose moralism is conditioned by Christianity.

The German professor does not play so essential a role. He is a strange mixture of pedantry and confused idealism. High up in the Andes he wants to found a university and cultural center for which none of the natural prerequisites are present, and which would inevitably perish in that severe climate. He serves Wilder's purpose of reducing the ideology of progress *ad absurdum.* The same thing is done in the pessimistic maxims of Mrs. Wickersham: "From time to time everyone goes into an ecstasy about the glorious advance of civilization. . . ." [17]

The professor, it will be recalled, played a role for Wilder in *Our Town,* in which he pedantically gave a geographical, geological, and sociological classification of the small community. We find something similar with respect to Coaltown. Wilder stresses, with a little irony, that the local professors are actively engaged in research into the community's remote past history. The professors' knowledge is very exact and they are meritorious in research, but they are lacking in broadness of vision and cannot achieve an adequately detached world view.

Coaltown is the diametrical opposite of the ideology of progress. The local industry ceased to be profitable. Finally the town has all but folded up. The public offices have left it, and even the post office has gone so that its present inhabitants have to pick up their mail at an auxiliary post office. But even today Coaltown is still interesting and worth a novel, for as Dr. Gillies concludes, "Coaltown is everywhere." [18] There are no "Golden Ages" and "Dark Ages," as the historians are fond of saying, but simply the "oceanlike monotony," in which changes are brought about only by the weather.[19]

The point is provocatively overstated, and this is done deliberately. One is not supposed to find the unique object that is the mark of a "great story"; care is taken to see that this is so, despite the "mystery story" opening. Nor is the real hero (John Ashley) one of the novel's exciting characters, although he has become involved in a seemingly exciting incident. Wilder tells us that one of the reporters covering his trial wrote of him as "our uninteresting hero." [20] Later we are assured that he is "late-maturing" [21] and that the same is true of his children.[22] As he himself says at one point, he is a "family man" and nothing but a "family man." [23] But what kind of family head? He was "indifferent to the admiration or contempt of others." [24] In "orderly and disorderly life" [25] John Ashley is a failure, and in the eyes of the small town he had, in respect to finances—which were what really mattered—"been breaking one of the most implacable laws of civilization." [26] *The Eighth Day,* then, is something like a novel without a personal hero, the hero being the human race as manifested in its tribes and families.

Chapters Four and Five offer Wilder ample opportunity for a great flashback into the two families' history. In Chapter Four he tells of the founding of the Ashley family, telling the story in reverse order, so to speak. Ashley's courting of a girl of German descent and his "wedding" are described. Wilder concludes his character analysis with a family trait: "The Ashley children and the Lansing children certainly had energy of mind, but the Ashley children had something more: a quality of abstraction, an impersonal passion. Where did that come from—that freedom from self-reference?" [27]

The next chapter begins with the portrayal and analysis of that generation from which the "freedom from self-reference" came, and the tracing of this is carried further back into earlier generations. Mention is made of the two successful children Roger and Lily; we then learn that the public shows the successful Ashleys its favor; and the thread of narrative then goes back to events of earlier generations until we are near the beginning of American history in the seventeenth century.

In this chapter Americanism undergoes what may be called a positive evaluation filtered by self-irony. One asks oneself whether this is Wilder's own homecoming after so many excursions into the early history of humanity.

The evaluation is of a typically Wilderian kind. Within

the story it is encased in a manuscript entitled *America Through the Telescope,* written by a man who had emigrated to the Seine and to the Thames and acquired British nationality. The reader versed in the history of literature is for a moment taken aback, as reminiscences are awakened in him.

Wilder is probably aware of the merry game of tracing the family tree, and perhaps recalls all that can be made and has been made of this sort of thing. It is necessary in a way, but can be carried to excess. Thus he gives us a comic-ironic description of a family tree, its descendants, and their traits: "Beata was an exemplary student, though she was not interested in knowledge for its own sake (von Diehlen and Kellerman), an accomplished performer on the piano, a superb cook (von Diehlen). She gave all of herself to whatever task was set before her (Kellerman)." [28]

This chapter gives a relatively broad presentation of the social conditions. A local center is chosen, Hoboken, giving the opportunity to describe an entire part of the American population, and it is done with characteristically Wilderian touches. Not that German *lederhosen* and Alpine hats decorated with a "shaving brush" appear; but beer does, and so does its importance for the family enterprise. With real skill and a use of irony that is amazingly deft, our gaze is directed to the German part of the population, with its strengths and its weaknesses—the "respectability" that so often becomes comical, the pursuit of education (a striving that contains the seeds of pedantry and compulsion), and the interest in family history, the object of which is so often a legendary and doubtfully acquired *von* to prefix to the family name.

Bitter tones make themselves heard in the further course of this chapter, softened somewhat by the casual undertone, "Such is life." These tones are perhaps most distinct in the passage where John Ashley reflects that the great illusions about life's meaning are ended at forty, and that it is good if at that point the children are not yet old enough to notice the effect of disillusion on their parents, who now try to compensate for life's emptiness with dubious substitute achievements: the possession of material power which makes it possible for them to buy every kind of thing in life, and the boastings that lead to the general respect and esteem on which they now set so much value.

This chapter not only reflects a segment of the realistic novel; it also has a generalizing perspective that becomes a view of life.

Since at the end of the 1960's—as we have already noted—the period of the multivolume family novel is past, and since Wilder himself is probably inclined to regard such a purely family novel as boring, he offers certain generalizations that at times sound like maxims. Sometimes they simply appear in the text as individuals' reflections; at other times they introduce a chapter, so that they become almost deductive in character. Examples of such chapter beginnings are "Mysterious are the laws of sexual selection. Ashley chose Beata to be his wife . . ." [29] and "There is a theory . . . that gifted children inherit from their grandparents, that talents skip a generation. . . . The Ashley and the Lansing children certainly had. . . ." [30] Important as the maxims are for knowing the general train of thought, they can on the other hand be enlarged at the cost of the story. This is especially true of the earlier chapters. One of the weaknesses of *The Eighth Day* is that the author has involuntarily let didacticism creep into his novel. Here the wisdom of age has perhaps made itself somewhat too independent.

The organization of the sequence and course of the individual chapters is at times rather evident. Also, the very fact of the varied descent of the Ashley and Lansing families gives rise to the suspicion that Wilder has relapsed into nineteenth-century dogmatic ways of thought according to which heredity and environment have become clearly defined factors. Wilder, with self-irony, speaks of these ideas as "teasers."

The opening of the next-to-last chapter is largely dominated by the family history of the Lansings, and already in the first sections the reader stops short as a maxim again occurs: "We keep saying that we 'live our lives.' Shucks! Life lives us." [31] Determinism? The accent here is hardly on determinism's nineteenth-century variants, but more on the idea that the individual's self-glorification cannot become too pronounced. That the above dictum can have a special meaning even in the Wilderian sense is clear from the variant statement, "God lives us." [32]

The chapter relating the Lansing family history takes its title from the wedding place of Breckenridge Lansing, just as the chapter on the Ashleys' history received its title from the name of John Ashley's wedding place. The chapter on the Lansings offers a Roman-American mixture; this naturally leads in turn to theories of heredity, which are received more with astonishment and irony than with scientific dogmatism. Darwin ("never tired of showing") is brought forward in evidence briefly and marginally, and so is old Dr. Gillies again, of whom it is said that he "worried ideas as a dog worries old bones" [33]—only to show in the end that nature always equalizes the extremes. In the historical examples he gives to support this thesis Wilder is not very exact. In the 1880's, when in fact no Polish state existed, he has a Polish warship with blond seamen arrive and create a balance in an area populated by dark-haired people.

Nevertheless, in his representation of various nations and races, Wilder is in a field familiar to American literature. Santayana in 1935 had already undertaken something similar in parts of *The Last Puritan*. In constructing his novel, however, Wilder had the opportunity to use the discussion of national character to make a typological comparison of the two family groups. Beata Ashley, the German girl, is called a "child of the ear," while Eustacia Lansing is the "child of the eye." Sound and color respectively govern the two women in their conduct and their forms of expression.

In this chapter Wilder must take up a certain amount of slack in regard to the detective-story aspect of the novel. We now learn that Breckenridge Lansing has a kind of—even if only desultory—assassination complex. We also learn more about the real murderer, George, who committed the murder in order to prevent something worse from happening.

Wilder returns to the subject of Breckenridge Lansing's father, who is in a sense the cause of the power complex that has appeared in his son and grandson. Old Lansing treated his wife and children with contempt, and his son at least attempted to do the same with his. Wilder softens the effect of this by adding that "this view was not universal in those States, but frequent." [34]

For Wilder the turn of the century saw the old patriarchal age approaching its end. Here too is one of Wilder's favorite themes—who does not remember that this same idea was the great provocative note in his speech on the occasion of his receiving the German book industry's Peace Prize?

Wilder suspects that the family's patriarchal order has its reflection in the realm of politics. The king, like the father, was endowed with divine attributes. Even bad kings were the expression of God's will: "Bad kings were sent for the punishment, instruction and edification of men." [35]

The problems that were involved in the old theories of the state keep on haunting the lives of families. The result, in the family of the elder Lansings, is the "bullying father" and the "cowed mother." [36] The "cage-feeling" engenders revolt, and here it must be said for the champions of the patriarchal family philosophy that they conformed *bona fide* to a tradition. Wilder remarks ironically that "Lansing had set out to found that greatest of all institutions—a God-fearing American home." [37] In regard to the plot, this had no small influence on the fact that Breckenridge was regarded by the jurors in the 1902 trial as innocent.

The Epilogue shows the Ashleys at their Christmas family gathering. The picture of the father, which had been on the walls of every police station and post office—a point to which repeated reference is made in the novel [38]—has been removed from one of those posters and installed in its place in the home. Ashley thereby has, for the public also, ceased to be a criminal.

The brief Epilogue serves the external purpose of revealing the details of Ashley's liberation by the members of a sect in the reconstruction of whose church he had once taken a part. At the same time it serves to clarify certain matters of world outlook in which concepts of history and time play a role. Wilder does not share the "flowing" concept of time that is so much favored in modern literature. "It is only an appearance that time is a river. It is rather a vast landscape and it is the eye of the beholder that moves." [39] Corresponding to this are the beginnings of certain chapters: "Ranges beyond ranges of hills, plains and rivers," [40] "Hills beyond hills," [41] "Vista after vista . . . Range beyond range. . . ." [42] Once again Wilder accentuates the idea that there is only one history: "This is a history. . . . But there is only one history." [43] Naturally he does not regard this history as a time object; he conceives of it instead as a visual object: "History is one tapestry." [44] These words are elucidated by four pictures—years apart—

from the histories of the Ashley and Lansing families.[45] The visual factor is further underscored as Wilder asks the reader, "Do you see?"

But to be certain that the reader does not remain too much within the sphere of family history, Wilder immediately afterward adds Coaltown and Babylon.

It is in line with Wilder's view of history that man's range of experience enables him to comprehend only a hand's breadth of his environment.[46]

In an earlier passage Wilder had stated: "That is what life is—an unfolding." [47] This is now transformed at the end of the book, in a letter by Ashley: ". . . our lives be used in the unfoldment of God's plan." [48] Salvation in history is also stressed once again as not being dependent on a Messiah. It is expressly said that it was a mistake of the Jews and the Christians to believe in a one and only Messiah, for the Messiah is a possibility in many branches of humanity.

Wilder's last novel to date, which in its original structure presented the appearance of a mystery and crime novel, has become in the course of its development more a novel of a philosophy of life. Technically this is not possible without the employment of means proper to the writer of an auctorial type of novel. Wilder uses auctorial interjection; he assumes the role of the prescient narrator, even going so far as to make frequent reference to events lying far beyond the 1905 limit set in the chapter headings, and sometimes even to events thirty or forty years later. Auctorial, too, is the already mentioned use of maxims, which largely stem not from any of the characters but from the author himself. The auctorial technique employed by Wilder in this novel makes him—with the aid of humor and irony toward the characters—into one who knows more than they do, even if he does not "know better" than they. In contrast to the writers of many other auctorial novels, he avoids a conservatism that would cause him to stand out in contrast to his characters. In this way his narrative technique and his narrative content become in a certain sense harmonized.

Thornton Wilder—
a Biographical Sketch

THORNTON WILDER was born in the Midwest on April 17, 1897. Not many Midwestern traces are to be found in his writings, which is no great surprise considering that his father left his newspaper publishing business in 1906 to go to Hong Kong as American Consul General. During these early years young Thornton attended German schools in Hong Kong and Shanghai, public schools in Berkeley, California, the China Inland Mission School in Cheefoo, the Thacher School in Ojai, California, and graduated from the Berkeley High School in 1915.

In 1915 he was enrolled at Oberlin College, and in 1917, following a family tradition, initiated by his father, he commenced his studies at Yale. Eight months of his junior year were spent in the coast artillery in World War I. Early writings of his appeared in the Yale literary magazine, and in 1920 he received his B.A. degree from Yale College. Not far from the university he had the house built in which he still lives today.

Two basic influences marked the first twenty-five years of his life. The fact that both his father and his mother were children of clergymen meant that he received a rich and profound religious education. On the other hand, the interest he had in Greek and Roman culture while at the university was furthered by a grant that he received to study at the American Academy in Rome.

His first novel, *The Cabala,* appeared in 1926, and was followed in 1927 by *The Bridge of San Luis Rey,* which received the Pulitzer Prize. Meanwhile his interest in the theater was showing itself in the small plays that he produced in these years. After extensive travel his next novel, *The Woman of Andros,* appeared in 1930. He lectured one semester of each year at the University of Chicago, and is active in academic life today.

After many attempts at playwriting, he had his first big success in 1938 with *Our Town,* which brought him the Pulitzer Prize for the second time.

The work of revising, adapting, and staging the plays of other authors led him into the field of the Vienna Volkstheater and to writing an adaptation of a farce by Nestroy. This was staged in 1938 under the title *The Merchant of Yonkers,* and was produced in somewhat modified form at the 1954 Edinburgh Festival under the title *The Matchmaker.*

In 1942 appeared his experimental play, *The Skin of Our Teeth,* which won him the Pulitzer Prize a third time and confirmed his literary fame.

Wilder's place among the recognized personalities of the Anglo-American literary world was again underlined in 1955 with the world premiere of his play *A Life in the Sun.* His dramatic work, which continues to hold a secure place in the theatrical repertoire, has won further interest as a result of Hindemith's opera based on Wilder's play *The Long Christmas Dinner* and of the production in Frankfurt of an opera based upon *A Life in the Sun.*

Bibliography

I WORKS OF THORNTON WILDER

A Novels and Novellas:

The Cabala. New York: The Modern Library, 1926.
The Bridge of San Luis Rey. New York: Albert & Charles Boni, 1927. Awarded the Pulitzer Prize.
The Woman of Andros. New York: Boni, 1930.
Heaven's My Destination. London: Longmans, Green & Co., 1934. New York: Harper & Bros., 1935.
The Ides of March. New York: Harper & Bros., 1948.

B Dramas

The Angel That Troubled the Waters: Three-Minute Plays for Three People. New York: Coward-McCann, 1928. Contents: *Nascuntur Poetae . . . , Proserpina and the Devil, Brother Fire, Childe Roland to the Dark Tower Came, The Angel on the Ship, Centaurs, Leviathan, And the Sea Shall Give Up Its Dead, Now the Servant's Name Was Malchus, Mozart and the Grey Steward, Hast Thou Considered My Servant Job?, Flight Into Egypt, The Angel That Troubled the Waters.*
The Long Christmas Dinner, and Other Plays in One Act. New York: Coward-McCann, 1931. Contents: *The Happy Journey to Trenton and Camden, The Long Christmas Dinner, Love and How to Cure It, Pullman Car Hiawatha.*
Our Town. New York: Coward-McCann, 1938. Awarded the Pulitzer Prize. German text: *Unsere kleine Stadt.* First performance: Princeton, N. J., January 22, 1938.

The Skin of Our Teeth. New York: Harper & Bros., 1942. Awarded the Pulitzer Prize. First performance: New York, November 18, 1942.
The Matchmaker (original version: *The Merchant of Yonkers*, 1938). In *Three Plays* (with *Our Town* and *The Skin of Our Teeth*). New York: Harper & Bros., 1957. First performance: New York, December 28, 1938.
A Life in the Sun. The Drunken Sisters. (Unpublished.) German text published under the title, *Die Alkestiade. Schauspiel in drei Akten mit einem Satyrspiel: Die beschwipsten Schwestern* ("The Alcestiad: A Play in Three Acts, with a Satyr Play, The Drunken Sisters"). Transl. H. E. Herlitschka. Fischer Bücherei series, No. 320, 1960. First performance: Edinburgh, August 24, 1955. First German language performance: Zurich, June 27, 1957. First performance in Germany: Frankfurt am Main, October 5, 1957.

II SELECTED BIBLIOGRAPHY ON THORNTON WILDER

Brown, E. K. "A Christian Humanist." In *University of Toronto Quarterly*, April 1935.
Burbank, Rex. *Thornton Wilder.* New York, 1961.
Campbell, Joseph, and Robinson, H. M. "The Skin of Whose Teeth?" In *Saturday Review of Literature*, December 19, 1942; February 13, 1943.
Edelstein, J. M. *A Bibliographical Checklist of the Writings of Thornton Wilder.* New Haven: Yale University Library, 1959.
Fergusson, Francis. "Three Allegorists: Brecht, Wilder and Eliot." In *Sewanee Review*, 1956.
Firebaugh, Joseph J. "The Humanism of Thornton Wilder." In *Pacific Spectator*, Fall 1950.
Fuller, Edmund. "Thornton Wilder: The Notation of a Heart." In *American Scholar*, Spring 1959.
Grebanier, Bernard. *Thornton Wilder.* University of Minnesota Press, 1964 (University of Minnesota Pamphlets on American Writers, No. 34).
Guthrie, Tyrone. "The World of Thornton Wilder." In *The New York Times Magazine*, November 27, 1955.
Hamburger, Käte. *Von Sophokles zu Sartre. Griechische Dramenfiguren antik und modern.* Stuttgart: Kohlhammer, 1962. See especially Chapter 6 on the figure of Alcestis.

Kesting, Marianne. *Das epische Theater.* Stuttgart: Kohlhammer, 1959 (Urban-Bücher series, No. 36). See pp. 106ff. on Wilder's dramas.

Kohler, David. "Thornton Wilder." In *The English Journal,* 1939.

Szondi, Peter. *Theorie des modernen Dramas.* Frankfurt am Main: Suhrkamp. 1956 (reprinted 1963 as No. 27 in the Edition Suhrkamp series). See especially Chap. 16 and 17.

Notes

CHAPTER 1: *The Cabala*

1 *The Cabala* (New York: The Modern Library, 1929) , p. 66.
2 *Ibid.,* p. 187.
3 *Ibid.,* p. 15.
4 *Ibid.,* p. 218.
5 *Ibid.,* p. 225.
6 *Ibid.,* p. 58.
7 *Ibid.,* p. 88.
8 *Ibid.,* pp. 127ff.
9 *Ibid.,* p. 158.
10 *Ibid.,* p. 179.
11 *Ibid.,* p. 227.
12 *Ibid.,* p. 145.
13 *Ibid.,* p. 198.
14 *Ibid.,* p. 222.
15 *Ibid.,* p. 225.
16 *Ibid.,* p. 228.
17 *Ibid.,* pp. 228f.
18 *Ibid.,* p. 227.
19 *Ibid.*
20 *Ibid.*
21 *Ibid.,* p. 229.
22 *Ibid.,* pp. 225ff.
23 *Ibid.,* p. 104.
24 *Ibid.*
25 *Ibid.,* p. 229.
26 *Ibid.*
27 *Ibid.*
28 *Ibid.,* p. 230.
29 *Ibid.,* pp. 42ff.

CHAPTER 2: *The Bridge of San Luis Rey*

1 In this tautness the work offers a good example of the way Wilder adopts European material for his own uses. Cf. Walther Fischer, "Thornton Wilders *The Bridge of San Luis Rey* und Prosper Mérimées *Le Carosse du Saint-Sacrement*"

(*Anglia,* Vol. 60, pp. 234–240) , which shows how Wilder makes of Mérimée's story a new work in which the personal names are almost the only thing retained.

2 Thornton Wilder, *The Bridge of San Luis Rey,* pp. 11, 32, 116 i.a. (Quotations are from the Penguin edition, London, 1941) .

3 *Ibid.,* p. 11.

4 *Ibid.,* p. 112.

5 "I am alone, alone, alone" (*Ibid.,* p. 74) .

". . . I am alone. Why have I never seen that before? I am alone" (Wilder, *The Woman of Andros,* New York, 1930; p. 40) .

". . . Do not leave me alone. Do not leave me so long alone" (*Ibid.,* p. 144) .

". . . do not leave me" (Wilder, *The Ides of March,* London, 1948; p. 45) .

6 Wilder, *The Angel That Troubled the Waters* (London: Longmans, Green & Co., 1928) , p. 70.

7 *Bridge,* pp. 114f.

8 *Ibid.,* p. 18.

9 *The Woman of Andros,* p. 128.

10 *Bridge,* p. 9.

11 *Ibid.,* p. 38.

12 *Ibid.,* p. 114.

13 *Ibid.,* p. 11.

14 *Ibid.,* p. 36.

15 *Ibid.,* p. 45.

16 *Ibid.,* p. 14.

17 *Ibid.,* p. 28.

18 *Ibid.,* p. 19.

19 *Ibid.,* p. 38.

20 *Ibid.,* p. 122.

21 *Ibid.,* p. 41.

22 *Ibid.,* p. 42.

23 Cf. also E. K. Brown, "A Christian Humanist: Thornton Wilder," *University of Toronto Quarterly* IV (April 1935) .

24 *Bridge,* p. 48.

25 *Ibid.,* pp. 18f.

26 *Ibid.,* p. 51.

27 *Ibid.*

28 *Ibid.,* p. 52.

29 *Ibid.,* p. 51.

30 *Ibid.,* p. 15.

31 *Ibid.,* p. 71.

32 *Ibid.,* p. 95.

33 *Ibid.,* p. 96.

34 *Ibid.,* p. 100.

35 *Ibid.,* p. 102.

36 *Ibid.,* p. 124.

37 *Ibid.,* p. 118.

38 *Ibid.,* p. 124.

39 *Ibid.*

40 *Ibid.,* p. 87.

41 *The Angel That Troubled the Waters* (New York, 1928) , p. xiv.

CHAPTER 3: *The Woman of Andros*

1 *The Woman of Andros* (New York: Albert & Charles Boni, 1930) , p. 7.
2 *Ibid.*, p. 162.
3 *Ibid.*, p. 7.
4 *Ibid.*, p. 8.
5 *Ibid.*, pp. 8f.
6 *Ibid.*, p. 9.
7 *Ibid.*, p. 159.
8 *Ibid.*, pp. 159f.
9 *Ibid.*, p. 90.
10 *Ibid.*, p. 148.
11 *Ibid.*, p. 118.
12 *Ibid.*, p. 117.
13 *Ibid.*, pp. 44f.
14 *Ibid.*, p. 84.
15 *Ibid.*, p. 33.
16 *Ibid.*, p. 37.
17 *Ibid.*, p. 35.
18 *Ibid.*, p. 99.
19 *Ibid.*, p. 39.
20 *Ibid.*, p. 86.
21 *Ibid.*, p. 96.
22 *The Angel That Troubled the Waters* (New York, 1928) , pp. 108f.
23 *The Woman of Andros,* p. 80.
24 *Ibid.*, p. 98.
25 *Ibid.*, pp. 98f.
26 *Ibid.*, p. 78.
27 Wilder's dependence on Terence, to which he himself makes reference, concerns especially the cast of characters; it concerns less the all-too-comic complications of Terence's plots.

Of Wilder's deviations from Terence the following are no table: (1) Wilder has shifted Chrysis to the center of the story; Terence's equivalent of Chrysis is a marginal figure; (2) the constellation of characters has been simplified; that is, Wilder has not made use of the secondary plot Philumela-Charinus and in place of Philumela makes Chrysis the sister of Glycerium; (3) the setting has been shifted from Athens to the imaginary island of Brynos.

CHAPTER 4: *Heaven's My Destination*

1 *Heaven's My Destination* (London: Longmans, Green & Co., 1934) , p. 211.
2 *Ibid.*, p. 159.
3 *Ibid.*, p. 113.
4 *Ibid.*, p. 199.
5 *Ibid.*, p. 37.
6 *Ibid.*, pp. 5, 23, 92.

7 *Ibid.*, p. 202.

8 *Ibid.*, pp. 165, 175.

9 *Ibid.*, p. 4.

10 *Ibid.*, p. 6.

11 *Ibid.*, p. 188.

12 *Ibid.*, p. 68.

13 *Ibid.*, p. 212.

CHAPTER 5: *The Ides of March*

1 *The Ides of March* (New York: Harper & Bros., 1948), Document 21, pp. 59ff.

2 *Ibid.:* Document 46 C, pp. 139f.

3 *Ibid.*, Document 64 A, p. 180.

4 *Ibid.*, p. 54.

5 *Ibid.*, pp. 41f.

6 *Ibid.*, pp. 2f.

7 *Ibid.*, p. 11.

8 *Ibid.*, p. 12.

9 *Ibid.*, p. 24.

10 *Ibid.*, p. 29.

11 *Ibid.*

12 *Ibid.*, p. 30.

13 *Ibid.*, p. 31.

14 *Ibid.*, p. 37.

15 *Ibid.*, p. 119.

16 *Ibid.*, p. 124.

17 *Ibid.*, p. 125.

18 *Ibid.*, p. 134.

19 *Ibid.*

20 *Ibid.*, p. 136.

21 *Ibid.*, p. 174.

22 *Ibid.*, p. 192.

23 *Ibid.*, p. vi.

24 *Faust*, Part II, Act I, 1. 6271ff.

25 *Ides*, p. 26.

26 *Ibid.*, p. 52.

27 *Ibid.*, p. 82.

28 *Ibid.*, p. 53.

29 *Ibid.*, p. 54.

30 *Ibid.*

31 *Ibid.*

32 *Ibid.*, p. 106.

33 *Ibid.*, p. 66.

34 *Ibid.*, pp. 67f.

35 *Ibid.*, p. 70.

36 *Ibid.*

37 *Ibid.*, p. 186.

38 *Ibid.*, pp. 147f.

39 *Ibid.*, p. 186.

40 *Ibid.*, p. 87.

41 *Ibid.*, p. 148.

42 *Ibid.*, p. 123; cf. also pp. 2ff. and 37.

43 *Ibid.*, p. 11.

44 *Ibid.*, p. 45.

45 *Ibid.*, p. 82.

46 *Ibid.*, p. 44.

47 *Ibid.*, p. 48.

48 *Ibid.*, p. 80.

49 *Ibid.*, pp. 106f.

50 *Ibid.*, vide p. 39.

51 *Ibid.*, p. 44.

52 *Ibid.*, p. 109.

53 *Ibid.*, p. 153.

54 *Pacific Spectator* IV, Autumn 1950, p. 426.

55 *Ibid.*, p. 168.

CHAPTER 6: *Our Town*

1 Grenville Vernon, "The Stage and the Screen." In *The Commonweal,* Vol. 28, p. 161 (June 1938).

2 Ima H. Herron, *The Small Town in American Literature* (Durham, N. C.: 1939).

3 Thornton Wilder, *Three Plays, With a Preface* (London and New York: 1958), p. vii.

4 *Ibid.,* p. xiii.

5 *Our Town* (New York, 1938), pp. 9f.

6 *Ibid.,* p. 10.

7 *Ibid.,* p. 57.

8 *Ibid.,* pp. 88f.

9 *Ibid.,* pp. 26, 38.

10 Ross Parmenter in *The Saturday Review of Literature,* XVIII 7, June 1938, p. 10.

11 Peter Szondi, *Theorie des modernen Dramas* (Frankfurt am Main; 1956), p. 65.

12 *Our Town,* p. 70.

13 *Ibid.,* p. 56.

14 *Ibid.,* p. 40.

15 *Ibid.,* p. 12.

16 In the case of a secondary character like the milkman, the lack of personal quality is suggested by the spoken sound of the name. Howie Newsome is "How we knew some" (page 15). Perhaps this is not meant to emphasize any particular "facelessness" in this person; rather the words "how we knew some" may apply to man in general.

17 *Ibid.,* p. 98.

18 *Ibid.,* p. 112.

19 *Ibid.*

20 *Ibid.,* pp. 125f.

21 *Ibid.,* p. 101.

22 *Ibid.,* p. 102.

CHAPTER 7: *The Skin of Our Teeth*

1 *The Skin of Our Teeth* (New York, 1942), p. 135.

2 Cf. especially the articles in the *Saturday Review of Literature* for the year 1943.

3 Genesis II, 18; *Skin of Our Teeth,* p. 2.

4 *Our Town,* p. 54.

5 *The Skin of Our Teeth,* p. 140.

6 *Ibid.,* p. 3.

7 *Ibid.,* p. 4.

8 *Perspektiven,* Vol. I, p. 103.

9 *Ibid.,* p. 103.

10 For the reference to Goethe's use of "Supplieren," I am obliged to my colleague Herr Boeckmann.

11 Thornton Wilder, *The Merchant of Yonkers.*

12 *Perspektiven,* Vol. I, p. 101.

13 *The Skin of Our Teeth,* p. 47.

14 *Ibid.,* p. 67.

15 *Ibid.,* p. 123.

16 *Ibid.,* p. 127.

17 *Ibid.,* p. 130.

18 *Ibid.,* p. 126.

19 *Ibid.,* p. 141.

20 *Ibid.,* p. 3.

21 *Ibid.,* p. 11.

22 *Ibid.,* p. 125.

23 *Ibid.,* p. 102.

24 *Ibid.*

25 *Ibid.,* p. 37.

26 *Ibid.,* p. 140.

27 *Ibid.,* p. 17.

28 Apocalypse I, 8.

29 *The Skin of Our Teeth,* p. 6.

30 *Ibid.,* p. 17.

31 *Ibid.,* p. 85.

32 *Ibid.,* p. 130.

33 *Ibid.,* p. 7.

34 *Ibid.*

35 *Ibid.*

36 *Ibid.,* p. 142.

CHAPTER 8: *Short Plays*

1 *The Angel That Troubled the Waters* (London: Longmans, Green & Co., 1928), Foreword, p. x.

2 *Ibid.,* p. 11.

3 *Ibid.,* p. 86.

4 Cf. Albert Köstler, *Das Bild an der Wand* (The Picture on the Wall), 1909.

5 Shakespeare, *King Lear,* III, 4, 187.

6 Revelation, XX, Chap. 5, Verse 13.

7 *The Angel That Troubled the Waters,* p. 47.

8 *Ibid.,* p. 93.

9 *Ibid.,* p. x.

10 John, V, 2 ff.

11 *The Angel That Troubled the Waters,* p. 106.

12 *Ibid.,* p. 82.

13 *Ibid.,* p. 86.

14 *Ibid.,* p. 87.

15 Joshua, VIII, 8; Numbers, XXI, 28.

16 Revelation, Book XX, Chap. 10, Verse 14 and Book XXI, Chap. 8.

17 *The Angel That Troubled the Waters,* p. 26.

18 *Ibid.*

19 *Ibid.,* p. 36.

20 *Ibid.*

21 *Ibid.,* p. 37.

22 *Ibid.,* p. 38.

23 *Ibid.,* p. 97.

24 *Ibid.,* p. 99.

25 *Ibid.,* p. 98.

26 *Ibid.,* p. 100.

27 *Ibid.,* p. 99.

28 *Ibid.*

29 *Ibid.,* p. 77.

30 *Ibid.,* p. 105.

31 *Ibid.,* p. 106.

32 *Ibid.,* p. 107.
33 *Ibid.,* p. 56.
34 *The Long Christmas Dinner* (London: Longmans, Green & Co., 1931) , p. 3.
35 *Ibid.,* pp. 5, 12f, 15.

36 *Ibid.,* pp. 56f.
37 *Ibid.,* p. 58.
38 *Ibid.,* p. 64.
39 *Ibid.,* p. 113.
40 *Ibid.*
41 *Ibid.,* p. 72.

CHAPTER 9: *A Life in the Sun*

1 Thornton Wilder's brother, Amos Wilder, informs me that an American text is not to be expected soon, owing to other projects on which the author is currently engaged. The quotations from *A Life in the Sun* are from the German edition published by Fischer Verlag. The quotations from the *Alcestis* are taken from the German translation by Hans von Arnim, published by Artemis Verlag, Zurich, 1958.
2 *The Woman of Andros* (New York, 1930) , p. 57.
3 *The Ides of March,* pp. 56f.
4 Plato, *Symposium* (German edition, Frankfurt am Main: Fischer Bücherei, 1960) , p. 179.
5 *A Life in the Sun,* pp. 12f.
6 *Ibid.,* p. 118.
7 For this reference as for other references to the Greek drama, I am indebted to my colleague Albrecht Dihle.
8 Euripides, *Alcestis,* line 381. The half line has been omitted from the German translation.

9 *Ibid.,* line 390.
10 *Ibid.,* line 297.
11 I am indebted to Dr. Inge Leimberg for first pointing out this connection.
12 What is involved here is above all line 684 of the *Alcestis.* In the two words "custom" and "law" are contained the debate of Euripides' time. What is here called "custom" may also refer instead to that which common sense requires.
13 Euripides, *Alcestis,* V, lines 681–691.
14 *Ibid.,* lines 38–45.
15 *Ibid.,* lines 60–63.
16 *A Life in the Sun,* p. 73.
17 *Ibid.,* p. 11.
18 *Ibid.,* p. 15.
19 *Ibid.,* p. 9.
20 *Ibid.,* p. 11.
21 *Ibid.,* pp. 12f.
22 *Ibid.,* p. 24.
23 *Ibid.,* p. 23.
24 *Ibid.,* pp. 23f.
25 *Ibid.,* pp. 39f.
26 *Ibid.,* p. 41.
27 *Ibid.,* p. 56.

28 *Ibid.*, p. 37.

29 *The Bridge of San Luis Rey,* p. 12.

30 *A Life in the Sun,* p. 37.

31 *Ibid.*, p. 14.

32 *Ibid.*, p. 56.

33 *Ibid.*, p. 12.

34 *Ibid.*, p. 14.

35 *Ibid.*, p. 28.

36 *Ibid.*, p. 33.

37 *Ibid.*, p. 41.

38 *Ibid.*, p. 42.

39 *Ibid.*, p. 97.

40 *Ibid.*, pp. 88f.

41 *Ibid.*, p. 113.

CHAPTER 10: *The Eighth Day*

1 *The Eighth Day* (New York, 1967), p. 18.

2 *Ibid.*, p. 10.

3 Chap. II and III.

4 *Ibid.*, p. 3.

5 *Ibid.*

6 *Ibid.*, p. 142.

7 *Ibid.*, p. 146.

8 *Ibid.*, pp. 153–54.

9 *Ibid.*, p. 249.

10 *Ibid.*, p. 106.

11 *Ibid.*, p. 107.

12 *Ibid.*

13 *Ibid.*, p. 108.

14 *Ibid.*, p. 123.

15 *Ibid.*, p. 124.

16 *Ibid.*, p. 165.

17 *Ibid.*, p. 198.

18 *Ibid.*, p. 18.

19 *Ibid.*

20 *Ibid.*, p. 5.

21 *Ibid.*, p. 122.

22 *Ibid.*, p. 146.

23 *Ibid.*, p. 114.

24 *Ibid.*, p. 32.

25 *Ibid.*, p. 126.

26 *Ibid.*, p. 34.

27 *Ibid.*, pp. 293–94.

28 *Ibid.*, p. 297.

29 *Ibid.*, p. 288.

30 *Ibid.*, p. 293.

31 *Ibid.*, p. 309.

32 *Ibid.*, p. 367.

33 *Ibid.*, p. 317.

34 *Ibid.*, p. 326.

35 *Ibid.*

36 *Ibid.*, p. 327.

37 *Ibid.*, p. 351.

38 *Ibid.*, pp. 32, 81, 90.

39 *Ibid.*, p. 395.

40 *Ibid.*, p. 397.

41 *Ibid.*, p. 401.

42 *Ibid.*, p. 420.

43 *Ibid.*, p. 395.

44 *Ibid.*, p. 396.

45 *Ibid.*

46 *Ibid.*, p. 435.

47 *Ibid.*, p. 379.

48 *Ibid.*, p. 428.